UNCHANGING POINTS OF LIGHT

*Finding Your Way
in the Dark*

EDWIN A. MCDONALD, III

Clovercroft Publishing

Unchanging Points of Light

© 2017 Edwin A. McDonald III

Published by Clovercroft Publishing, Franklin, Tennessee

Published in association with Larry Carpenter of
Christian Book Services, LLC of Franklin, Tennessee

Scripture quotations marked (ESV) are from the ESV® Bible (The Holy Bible, English Standard Version®), copyright © 2001 by Crossway, a publishing ministry of Good News Publishers. Used by permission. All rights reserved.

Scripture taken from THE HOLY BIBLE, NEW INTERNATIONAL VERSION®, NIV® Copyright © 1973, 1978, 1984, 2011 by Biblica, Inc.™ Used by permission. All rights reserved worldwide.

Scripture taken from the NEW AMERICAN STANDARD BIBLE®, Copyright © 1960, 1962, 1963, 1968, 1971, 1972, 1973, 1975, 1977, 1995 by The Lockman Foundation. Used by permission.

Edited by Robert Irvin

Cover and Interior Design by Suzanne Lawing

ISBN: 978-1-942557-80-7

Printed in the United States of America

CONTENTS

DEDICATION

This book is dedicated to my family.

To my parents, Ed and Carol McDonald. They weren't perfect, but their love and support were relentless. They taught me so much, and gave me so much that endures.

To my sister Vicki and brother-in-law Mike. Your devotion to me is not based on objectivity. Rather, it flows from the irrational experience of love. You are the best!

To my son, Ashton. I have learned more by being your dad than all the books, classes, lectures, and sermons I have experienced. You make it all worthwhile. You are the best thing that ever happened to me.

To my friends who are essentially my family as well. You have been by my side, regardless. You didn't have to be there. You will never know how much that means to me.

All of you have brought life to my life when I most needed it. Thank you for believing in me.

ACKNOWLEDGMENTS

Unchanging Points of Light is a book of ideas. They did not begin with me. There are so many people who have contributed to this book in so many ways. Mostly, they do not know. One person who does know is Bob Irvin, my editor. You made an impossible task possible. Thank you.

My professional coach and good friend, Dr. Joel Small, encouraged me to chase my dream of writing this book. Thank you, Joel. You inspire me.

The books, CDs, and web-based resources that have shaped my thoughts are too many to list. There are a number of people who have served and continue to serve as world-class teachers to me. To all of you, I say thank you from the bottom of my heart. The list begins with these people.

- Buddy Liles of Allen Bible Church. You teach and lead with an authentic and loving heart. Your life is a living, breathing testimony. When you preach the gospel, occasionally you use words. You are a wise and gentle shepherd.

- Ravi Zacharias has been my teacher for more than a decade. I have spent hundreds and hundreds of hours with him by CD and the online versions of RZIM. Ravi provides amazing insight on apologetics and philosophy to people all over the world. Ravi, your life and work is a testimony. In addition, at Ravi Zacharias International Ministries, Michael Ramsden, Amy Orr-Ewing, John Lennox, and Nabeel Qureshi have expanded my capacity to engage and advance the ideas presented in this book.

- Tom Nelson of Denton Bible Church, Todd Wagner of Watermark Church in Dallas, and Tim Keller of Redeemer Presbyterian Church in New York City collectively have provided hundreds of hours of instruction to me as well as amazing examples of the church serving the community. I have listened to your sermons and teachings so many times in an effort to grasp their deeper meanings. They provided a foundation for this book and grew my efforts to understand what God has declared to all of us.

- Finally, Matt Chandler of The Village Church in Highland Village has been a constant source of unique, honest, energetic, and extremely entertaining teaching. Your messages direct me to pathways of hope. In fact, I almost have the "I Am" series of 2016 memorized! I do not have words to express my gratitude.

WHY 'UNCHANGING POINTS OF LIGHT'?

For as long as I can remember, I have loved learning. I hope and plan that on the last day of my life, I will be learning. What drives me is the need, the desire, to understand the world around me. That drive includes both the natural world and the supernatural world.

I graduated with a BS in chemistry from Midwestern State University in Wichita Falls, Texas. In many ways, Midwestern was an ordinary, small state university. For me, it was anything but ordinary. One extraordinary person in those four years was my organic chemistry professor and advisor, Eldon H. Sund, PhD. I would not have made it without his guidance and sincere interest in my education and development. As Dr. Sund's student, and working in his lab, I received a foundation in scientific methodology and the importance of objectivity in scientific research. That objectivity is often a missing element in today's world. We just don't see clearly. We often don't think objectively.

In writing on some of the most important subjects in our world, it was important to me to develop ideas that were grounded in sound science and consistent with the laws of logic. That sounds like a strange thing to say in 2017, but so many ideas that we routinely accept and believe are anything but that. I hope and believe that you will find new ways to view the world and its important issues through this book.

In addition, I am a baby boomer who grew up in the 1960s, a time of great awakening that included multiple social revolutions. I was a part of that period of upheaval! As the "revolutionaries" of the 1960s matured, we began to experience consequences and implement responses to the actions we took. Most people began to experience a great deal of angst as they witnessed and experienced all of this change.

I was included in that group.

* * * * * * *

What do you hang on to when you are lost? I mean really lost. When everything you thought was real has dissolved. When what you have believed in is just gone. When the structure of your life is broken. Many years ago, those questions came to life for me. In the middle of a very significant counseling session, the clinical psychologist I was seeing stopped me mid-sentence as I was expressing dismay about the circumstances of my life and the decisions I had made to contribute to those same circumstances. He said: "Isn't it possible that God knew all of this was going to happen, that you were going to make these choices and that, in spite of any angst that you have, he loves you and has a plan for your life?" As obvious as that may seem to you, it wasn't obvious to me at the time! In that very emotional moment, my circumstances tipped. They did not tip away from problems, but they moved me back to the idea that there really could be a plan for my life that was above and beyond my circumstances. It gave me hope that there was something and someone I could lean on and count on through any and all of the challenges of my life. That I would never be alone again and, through His eyes, I might see clearly enough to find my way.

Hanging on to eternal and unchanging points of light, I did.

* * * * * * *

The changes in our culture have continued, expanded, and intensified over the last thirty to forty years to the point that some type of crisis seems inevitable, or perhaps even necessary, to reset the foundations of society. The sheer number and severity of actual and potential threats in our world appears, to me, to be at an unprecedented level. It also seems to me that our understanding of these threats is inadequate and incorrect.

These threats range from corruption to radical Islamic terrorism, the sovereign debt of nations, human trafficking, the conflict of nations as they struggle over geography, improper influence and mismanaged wealth, and climate change. Actually, those threats are just the beginning! All these things, taken as a whole, are beyond overwhelming—and they haunt me. I often think: What can one person do to make any difference?

A couple of years ago, I was having a conversation with a friend, Fred, about these very things and more. Among the "more" was a great deal of criticism for the ideology, strategies, and methodology of our elected officials, especially our Congress and President. In the election year of 2016 we were faced with very disappointing nominees for the highest office in the land. Outside of the hard-core supporters for each one, few people wanted to elect either of the two major party nominees. Some people decided not to vote. Some decided to just give up.

Fred asked me not to respond by giving up. I haven't. Instead, I wrote *Unchanging Points of Light*. It is my personal effort to push back the darkness and shine a very bright light on some of the biggest issues of our day. It is what I could do to make a difference. It is what some call the power of one.

This effort starts with a look at the *truth*. A devotion to the pursuit of truth is the commonality or unifying principle of people of differing views. Without it, we have a stagnant free-for-all.

It ends with a look at light. Where and how do we look for light in a dark world? Now, more than ever, we need illumination. We need clarity of the reality of our world. We need hope. It is the fuel of life. *Light* is always a metaphor for the goodness that brings hope.

In between, we will look at the tipping points of life and culture. The places that we really need to get right in order to heal . . . in order to be whole again.

I am a Christian. By definition, that means I believe that Jesus is who He claimed to be and that the Bible is true. Before you decide what that means, how that defines me and others who follow Jesus, I invite you to look at the rest of the story I present in the following chapters. It was written for seekers, skeptics, and believers. I have referenced many sources that agree—and disagree—with my positions.

It was written with all the heart I can generate. It comes from the place I feel the deepest about and for which I keep alive hope—until it hurts. In spite of my own failures, the darkness of our world, and man's inhumanity to man, I believe in you. That belief comes from the knowledge that you and I were created in the image of God and according to His likeness. You were made by Him in a distinct and unique manner for a specific purpose.

My hope is that the thoughts you find in this book will help you unlock and illuminate what you need to live out that purpose. If it does that in some way, small or big, then I will have succeeded.

ONE

TRUTH

"Then you will know the truth,
and the truth will set you free."
—JOHN 8:32 (NIV)

As I began this chapter, the 2016 election was in full force. I realize that to place a politician or the political process in a chapter on truth is to violate almost every standard of objectivity and reason! And yet, almost every statement from almost every candidate was scrutinized by some fact-check process—and then reported for the world to see. In a day and age when truth has been relegated to a moldable, flexible, and often-manipulated second-class state, human beings still need to know if public officials are telling the truth. And they *really* need to know if the most important people in their lives—their family, friends, and colleagues—are being truthful with them. Or that they have the intention of being truthful.

And to me, that begs the question: Can we be honest with

ourselves and one another without a well-developed foundation of truth in our lives and culture? I don't think so. I believe
we would have chaos, conflict, and confusion individually and
collectively. And to me, that sounds like the world we live in
today. If our lives individually and collectively are going to
gather the power necessary to do battle with the problems of
our day, then we have to get this right.

Our current state of affairs leads me to ask the obvious
question: Does truth exist, or is it an illusion? If it exists, then
what place does it occupy in our lives? In order to answer
these questions, I believe we need to decide what we mean by
truth. Before beginning this study, I believed this was a very
simple subject. That view was a reflection of my inadequate
understanding of the many views of truth and, quite frankly,
my naïveté. So what is the philosophical basis of truth, and
what are the historic developments that have affected the role
of truth in our lives?

The importance of pursuing truth became apparent to me
as an undergraduate student working for Dr. Eldon Sund, my
chemistry professor, in his laboratory. Dr. Sund had a grant
from the Robert Welch Foundation to do very specific research in organic chemistry. Under Dr. Sund's direction, we
would complete experiments and measure the results using
very exacting instrumentation. He would then evaluate the
results and compare them with his predicted models. Once a
year, he would formally present his findings to the foundation
and his peers. They all counted on him to be fair and objective in his reporting; they would rely on it for their work. If
Dr. Sund had manipulated the data in any way, it could be
damaging to their work and the overall body of knowledge in
chemistry. There was never a question about his objectivity or
credibility. It was just built in to his *ethic* and *professionalism*.
That standard is the foundation of all progress.

As a dental student and now a practicing dentist, the importance of truth has become even more apparent. A dentist

has very specific knowledge that is outside most people's expertise. Given that, I have an obligation to not only report the patient's conditions fairly and accurately, but also to consider them in light of the patient's circumstances and objectives and what I believe will best help them. If I lose sight of truly being in the business of helping my patients, then I have lost everything it means to be a professional. In other words, I need to consider the patient's interests prior to my own in order to serve them well. In addition, I need to consider the whole person in the recommendations and counsel I offer. Sadly, there are too many times a professional will choose to not act professionally and practice his or her profession focused on their own motivations and profitability. That is a setup to manipulate the truth and apply professional skills to benefit the practitioner instead of the patient.

> IF I LOSE SIGHT OF TRULY BEING IN THE BUSINESS OF HELPING MY PATIENTS, THEN I HAVE LOST EVERYTHING IT MEANS TO BE A PROFESSIONAL. IN OTHER WORDS, I NEED TO CONSIDER THE PATIENT'S INTERESTS PRIOR TO MY OWN IN ORDER TO SERVE THEM WELL.

In the very simple and practical matter of providing basic dental care to human beings, a devotion to truth matters. In fact, without that, how can I ever do the right thing for them? No one in my profession could. If there isn't a truth to conform myself to, how can anyone trust me with their health? That trust means everything. When I am treating complex dental problems, the importance of trust between the patient, doctor, and team is magnified.

* * * * * * *

Generally speaking, truth is considered to be that which bests describes reality or that which maintains fidelity to a standard or ideal. Each academic discipline has its own criteria of truth or methodology for evaluating truth claims. History, language, science, and medicine all have very unique and exacting methods of evaluating truth claims. Basically, if you are going to stand before an academy and make assertions, the academy will demand that you follow its standards in supporting your claims with evidence. Most will expect that you have compared your findings with peer-reviewed published literature, and that your assertions are grounded in the established standards of that profession.

The next question asks if truth is *subjective, objective, absolute,* or *relative.* A **subjective** view of reality includes a person's perceptions, experiences, expectations, cultural understanding, and beliefs that inform their view of truth or reality. An **objective** view of reality is free of any individual's influence upon it. So, an objective view says that something is true or false independent of a person's interpretations, feelings, or biases. The **absolute** view of truth is the concept of an unconditional reality that transcends limited, conditional, everyday existence. It represents a universal and unchanging standard or reference point from which to think, act, and live. In contrast, the **relative** view is a concept that takes into account changing cultural norms, contemporary ideas, and often popular yet poorly developed ideologies.

There are still more theories; bear with me for just a short section of exploring a few more. Socrates, Plato, Aristotle, and Aquinas held to the **correspondence** theory of truth while seeking to best describe reality. In essence, it says that the job of the individual is to conform to reality rather than attempting to conform reality to the individual and his or her views. A **coherence** theory attempts to relate a specific part to an entire system in the view that truth is primarily a property of the whole system. Spinoza and Hegel embraced this idea. **Constructivist** theory says that knowledge is "constructed" through social and cultural experiences. **Consensus** theory say that the majority view wins out in the struggle for truth. The **pragmatic** theory, developed by William James, says that truth is verified and confirmed by putting one's concepts into practice and then observing the actual results.[1]

The potential for conflict in the these competing views is obvious. However, there is commonality in them as well. In the end, we have to ask and answer the question: *What is the source of truth?* Does it come from the ideas of man, or is there a source beyond human capacity and origin? The answer to that central question will direct and ground most of your life, whether you realize it or not.

> IN THE END, WE HAVE TO ASK AND ANSWER THE QUESTION: *WHAT IS THE SOURCE OF TRUTH?* DOES IT COME FROM THE IDEAS OF MAN, OR IS THERE A SOURCE BEYOND HUMAN CAPACITY AND ORIGIN?

Finally, there is a historical timeline of thought and events that has influenced the concept of truth in the modern era. One commentator stated that all modern thought begins with Kant . . . meaning Immanuel Kant, the famous philosopher of the 1700s. Kant believed that human experience is a filter that affects our experience of truth and that reason is the source of morality. In essence, Kant believed that he was here to bring about a Copernican type of revolution to philosophy. (As you recall, Copernicus was the astronomer who established the Sun as the center of our solar system, rather than the earth. It got him in a lot of hot water with the religious authorities, but nonetheless, Copernicus was right.) Likewise,

Kant proposed that there is no such thing as reality, or a universal reality, for each individual to conform to; rather, there is only reality as it appears to you.

That central idea of each person constructing reality through their unique human filter is in full force today. It usually sounds something like this: "What is true for you is true for you. What is true for me is true for me." Or we simply approach *truth* as something that is subject to interpretation by each individual.

Fortunately, pilots, engineers, and surgeons don't approach their work like that, or we would be living and dying through a continuous epidemic of disasters. But, in essence, our divorce from the truth has set in motion an epidemic of social, cultural, and behavioral disasters.

Kant was just the first of many voices of "modernism." Charles Darwin would come along and start a revolution in science and scientific thought. His observations on the adaptations of the characteristics within a given species would be extrapolated into an explanation of the origin of life, and for the first time, his ideas provided a vehicle that could attempt to explain life separate from a Creator-God. That idea would also include a search for truth that did not view a Creator and Sustainer as the source of truth, but that enlightenment and knowledge would come from human discovery, education, and technology. These appear to be the central ideas of modernism. The abject failure of those ideas, however, would later give birth to post-modernism.

Frederick Nietzsche, a brilliant German philosopher, would become one of the most influential voices in modernism; he officially led the "God is dead" movement. Of course, God was not actually dead, but Nietzsche stated that the role of God in our lives and culture was dead. Interestingly, he was the son of a minister, and both of his grandfathers were ministers. His views contributed to dramatic changes of Western thought that brought about the decline of Christian belief in

Europe and the United States. As such, God as a source of truth was diminished in Western thought.

Currently, Western culture is in a dead sprint away from the position of God as being foundational in the lives of men and women and, in fact, there are enormous efforts to eliminate God from public life altogether. The movement to a totally secular and naturalistic view of the world has done nothing but expand since Nietzsche's death in 1900.

SINCE KANT GAVE US PERMISSION TO CREATE OUR OWN REALITY, MARX DID JUST THAT.

Adding to the development of modern thought was a call for social realignment. Karl Marx and friends identified an elite aristocracy that had been abusive of common men and women for most, if not all, of history. Marx viewed the aristocracy as the prime source of injustice in the world. As such, a radical reorientation of economic systems into what we now call communism was his solution to these economic and political injustices. Since Kant gave us permission to create our own reality, Marx did just that.

Marx also believed that changing the economic system of men and women would change them into better people. It didn't. Marxist ideas began to influence and impact intellectual thought and eventually governments around the world. With Nietzsche declaring God as dead and Darwin providing a mechanism that eliminated the need for a Creator-God, it was a perfect storm for Marx to propose and introduce a godless culture of socialistic/communistic ideology as a solution to the injustices of the world. The modernists believed in the promises of modernism. Simply stated, modernism promised that education and intellectual advancement, combined with technological revolution and a reordering of society, would combat the injustice wrought against the common man by the aristocracy; in so doing, it would produce better societies and better people. Instead, these modern ideas would create havoc for the next one hundred years as this ideology failed to produce the expected outcomes it had so passionately promised. What it actually produced was a transfer of power from the aristocracy to a new ruling elite class that wound up producing unprecedented human suffering. Instead of creating utopias, it created dystopias.

In fact, it was *Nietzsche* who predicted that, if he was correct in his assertion that God was truly dead, the twentieth century would become the bloodiest century in recorded history. And it was. Most estimates conclude that 100 million to 200 million people were murdered by their own governments in an effort to cleanse their nations of dissent. The carnage is a testimony to the profound error in Marx's ideology and his abandonment of objective and proven principles of human behavior in favor of an untested reality that he created.

In a similar sense, Victor Frankel, an Austrian psychiatrist who survived the Holocaust, wrote one of the seminal books of all time, *Man's Search For Meaning.* He said that the plans for the Holocaust were not drawn up in a Nazi war room, but rather in the classrooms of the university campuses by nihilist professors who, by definition, rejected all theories of religious and moral belief. Frankel said the ideas of modernism propagated by the intellectual elite of the day served as justification for man's brutal inhumanity to man. Ideas have consequences: in this case, horrific ones.

As the modern thought of Darwin, Nietzsche, Marx, and others was put into practice with disastrous results, disillusionment set in for many of its supporters. In that failure and cynicism, postmodern thought was born. It was not developed on precepts and principles, but rather birthed out of the despair of taking what was supposed to be the best of human thought and enlightenment and watching it fail miserably.

Postmodern thought has many well-known voices. Jean-

Paul Sartre, Albert Camus, Jacques Derrida, and others are just starting places for this list. One of the earliest voices was a brilliant Cambridge philosopher, Ludwig Josef Johann Wittgenstein. Wittgenstein influenced much of twentieth-century philosophy. He helped to begin a way of thinking that says reality is an illusion, and therefore any attempts to define it are futile. Rather than examining the error of modern thought and attempting corrections, the postmodernists simply gave up all efforts to reconcile men and women with the reality of their world and stated that reality doesn't exist. So why bother with the essential human experience that seeks understanding of origin, destiny, purpose, and morality?

With all of that lost, what remained was freedom and the pleasure of living without restraint. Sartre would say that it is forbidden to forbid. (An argument, by the way, if one thinks about it on the most basic level, that falls apart on itself!) Camus and others, in their own way, would say that total freedom was the ultimate end of man, and therefore the concept of an all-powerful Creator-God was not possible as it would introduce moral and ethical restraint. However, when one says yes to the idea of total freedom, he or she is saying no to the possibility of meaning and purpose for human life. If we exist as a random biochemical event without purpose built into us, how can there be meaning to life? All of the postmodern writers I have encountered admit this. In fact, many of them would say that accepting a meaningless life is essential to living well! Sartre would exhaust himself writing about the meaninglessness and nothingness of life as the obvious outcomes of losing both God and the eternity that accompanied him. So then, according to Sartre, Camus, Derrida, and others, living for pleasure becomes the chief aim of man. At the end of his life, after all of his writing and work, Sartre concluded that his philosophy was unlivable. One of his longtime companions thought that he had gone mad. I believe it is much more likely that he "sobered up," faced death, and just couldn't reconcile his ideology with the reality he was facing.

As the ideas of postmodern thought expanded through the writings of Camus, Derrida, and Michel Foucault, the impact on the college classroom of the twentieth century was significant. These ideas seemed to focus on language and morality. Camus, Derrida, and Foucault essentially asked this question: Do words and language have inherent meaning, or are they instruments of power that are used to expand particular views and ideologies by those with power? Their answer was, of course, that words have no inherent meaning. They also asked if there were objective standards of morality. Again, the answer was no. Remember, it is forbidden to forbid. Any and all behaviors must be allowed if they fit into the constructed reality of the individual. Along with that, and perhaps because of that, every belief system is to be granted equal value, regardless of the consequences and performance of those beliefs in the lives of men and women and the culture they are part of. Interestingly, in answering the question: Are there any absolutes?, it seems the postmodern answer is: absolutely not.

So the revolution was complete. God was dead. Meaning was lost. Morality was conditional. Man had crowned himself king and was sitting on the throne. But just as Sartre said, man was essentially ruling over bubbles of emptiness floating on a sea of nothingness. Does that sound like progress? Does it sound like a framework or foundation we can all unite behind to construct a better and more enlightened world where human beings flourish? In my view, it sounds more like chaos and conflict . . . which is exactly what we observe in our world today. And the frequency and severity of that chaos and conflict appear to be increasing at an alarming rate. Philosophical education does not often leave the college campus, but eventually the students do. Over time, the students of the last five decades grew to positions of influence and leadership, and they brought much of this philosophy with them.

In all of this, the role and importance of truth has diminished. Generally, but not universally, the culture of the West believes that each person determines truth for themselves. By definition, this means that there are many different versions of the truth that are supposed to be equally valid, regardless of any conflict that exists between the differing views. In fact, we have come to value what is called *diversity, plurality,* and *self-determinism* so much that we will abandon the laws of logic in order to accept the unavoidable conflicts that exist between the differing views!

To make all of this worse, certain cultural positions are protected from dissent and criticism, regardless of the current factual evidence or established history. These cultural positions include whatever is the current politically correct set of beliefs in the West . . . to the power of traditional beliefs that are passed on by the elders in an honor-shame type of Eastern culture . . . to the ever-relentless stream of self-deception that is alive and well in all of us. Postmodern thought muddies the waters even further by asserting that reality/truth is a mere illusion: "There is no such thing as truth." Or, "You can't legislate morality." However, a fundamental examination of law reveals that all laws are constructed on, around, or as a reflection of some moral/ethical truth concerning the affairs of men and women.

IN ALL OF THIS, THE ROLE AND IMPORTANCE OF TRUTH HAS DIMINISHED. GENERALLY, BUT NOT UNIVERSALLY, THE CULTURE OF THE WEST BELIEVES THAT EACH PERSON DETERMINES THE TRUTH FOR THEMSELVES.

So, what does truth look like in our postmodern world? To me it looks like the Occupy Wall Street movement. This movement began in September of 2011, just a few years after the near collapse of the world's financial system. It was protesting income inequality and the influence of large corporations and financial institutions on government and the lives of everyday citizens. It was built on the slogan "We are the 99 percent."[2] However, it was not organized into a specific structure with specific leaders. It had no stated objectives, methods, goals, or solutions. It did not offer a moral/ethical basis for its protest. However, it did point to the obvious greed and corruption present on Wall Street. In short, it assumed an anarchist style of thought and operation. So it was birthed from disillusionment with economic outcomes and dislike of greed and corruption, but the movement had no stated standards of truth, ethics, or morality.

In the 2016 election, this movement took on new life in the form of Democratic presidential candidate Bernie Sanders. Sanders was a very quick study. First, he had essentially no training or experience in leadership or the executive skill sets needed to be President of the United States. If legislative accomplishments are a standard to judge an elected official by, then Sanders had accomplished, essentially, nothing. Sanders objected to the greed and corruption in the investment banks of Wall Street. So do I. He objected to the cost of nearly all college educations. It is unsustainable, he said. I agree. But all he could offer was a bureaucratically stagnant, corrupt, and grotesquely ineffective federal government as the solution. Bernie Sanders was wildly popular with Generation Y and many others despite having absolutely no basis or methodology to accomplish his proposals.

So in this vacuum, where do we get the power needed for change? How do we develop the agents and methodology of change without a basis to establish what is just and a reflection of truth for all people? In short, you can't. In my view, postmodern thought is the equivalent of philosophical anarchy; it strips language of meaning and morality of the power needed to restrain evil. Greed, corruption, and power-driven human beings exist in all economic systems.

In the end, a transformation of the human heart is what is needed to restrain evil and produce a more just outcome for the 99 percent of society that does not live in the privileged class. To do that, individuals will have to painfully confront the reality of themselves in light of the truth of human experience . . . especially their own experience.

Standards are required by a civil society that seeks order, unity, and opportunity. So what happens when order is missing, inadequate, or undeveloped? Crisis. In 2008, it happened to Wall Street and the world's financial system. I will never forget the news alerts of 2008; among them, Bear Stearns was failing. One of the largest and most influential investment banks in the world was about to fail. That news sent the Federal Reserve Bank, the United States Treasury Department, the President, and all other investment bank executives into a panic about the possibility of Bear Stearns beginning a brutal and sequential run of bank failures and, possibly, the entire world banking system. How was this possible?

> STANDARDS ARE REQUIRED BY A CIVIL SOCIETY THAT SEEKS ORDER, UNITY, AND OPPORTUNITY. SO WHAT HAPPENS WHEN ORDER IS MISSING, INADEQUATE, OR UNDEVELOPED? CRISIS.

First, the idea of thrift and financial responsibility on the part of each individual had been replaced by indulgence. Bigger and more expensive houses, home furnishings, cars, clothes, and travel were accompanied by bigger debt loads for each individual and more risk to lenders and borrowers alike. So a standard of truth that would limit the debt and risk that an individual and an institution would take on was replaced by an expanding ethic of immediate gratification, entitlement, and irresponsibility. Of course, there are many circumstances that could put an individual in a financial crisis beyond their control. An unexpected medical crisis is the most common cause of personal bankruptcy. Even in health care, the financial trends were terrible. Modern medicine had expanded, by multiples, what was possible in treating disease and saving lives. At the same time, the cost of care had expanded greatly and benefits had diminished substantially, creating an ever-expanding affordability gap. Understandably, people want the best health care available. All of this added to the debt burden of many. In some cases, the mentality of entitlement fed these systems. And a sense of entitlement, in my view, is present at all income levels.

In summary, this crisis could not have occurred without widespread expansion of debt beyond what had been previously considered prudent. In essence, mortgage lenders would accept the greater risk of lending more money to home buyers based on the gamble that home prices would continue to rise. In 2005, home prices peaked and then fell. That put many homeowners in a personal financial crisis as their credit cards were maxed out and their savings minimal or nonexistent. As the economy faltered in 2008, many people lost jobs, their income fell, and as they were living paycheck to paycheck, the crisis deepened. It was painful.

What was needed with public and private financing was an understanding of basic elements of truth. Abandoning the truth eventually inflicts pain and suffering or, at a minimum, expands and intensifies the pain and suffering of our lives.

It wasn't just the consumer at fault here. The federal government played a key role in the crisis. In the 1990s our elected officials decided they wanted to expand home ownership to as many people as possible. By 2005, they had. To accomplish that, they used the governmental lending institutions of Fannie Mae and Freddie Mac to be the buyer of any and all mortgages regardless of the quality of the loan, capability of the borrower, or the underlying value of the real estate relative to the loan amount. In essence, the lenders could pass on the risk of the loan to those institutions and pocket the profits of making the loan. So they did.

The problem was that Fannie Mae and Freddie Mac became grossly insolvent and required massive governmental bailouts. Many of the borrowers became insolvent as well. They were just not capable of managing the mortgage debt they took on. Of course, no elected official was willing to admit that their policy of expanding home ownership as far as possible had disastrous results or that they had anything to do with it. Expanding home ownership is a noble objective. But as with all things, it still requires an objective view of reality, responsibility, and risk. The truth is relentless.

To complete the financial crisis, a great multiplier was needed. It just so happened that Wall Street had one ready. They called the multiplier a *derivative*. A magician would call it an illusion. My father, a Depression-era child, would simply say that there is no such thing as a free lunch. It turns out, he was right.

These derivatives were classified as mortgage-backed securities. Historically, a million dollars worth of real estate secured a million-dollar security, or something close to that value. It was a very secure investment. In a derivative, through a financial sleight of hand, a million dollars of real estate secures thirty million dollars of securities. This is, simply, a highly leveraged investment. When real estate values began to drop and the ability of debtholders to service their loans declined, you now had a full-tilt meltdown. Investment banks and other financial institutions quickly moved toward insolvency. Retirement and other important funds also took huge hits. All of this threatened the world's financial systems. It took extreme measures to prevent a collapse.

Why does all this belong in a chapter on truth? Wall Street is filled with the brightest of minds trained at the finest universities in the world. They are paid amazing amounts of money to lead and operate these critical institutions. But the universities that trained them long ago abandoned a belief in the truth. They believe and teach that truth is relative and determined by each individual. Also, in that view, truth is a work in progress as culture and its beliefs evolve from one popular idea to the next. That which had been historically established with decades or even centuries of real-world trial by fire in the marketplace now could be replaced by "modern thought"! As an example, see the Internet stock bubble of 2000, when historic price-to-earnings ratios were discarded. In essence, there was one absolute truth in place on Wall Street: profit at all costs. It was greed that ruled the Street. The greatest financial leaders in the United States, perhaps the world, put the entire financial system at risk just to earn a greater profit through the leveraging of junk securities. They knew better and did it anyway. The buyers should have known better than to believe you could get extremely high yields without extremely high risk.

In this case, there was nobody innocent. The consumer wanted more than he or she could afford or pay back. They were willing to put their personal financial condition at risk of insolvency just to indulge themselves. The federal government was willing to provide institutions to be used as the buyer of any and all mortgages regardless of their quality in order to execute a profoundly flawed ideology for political gain. The great multiplier was the greed that immoral and unethical Wall Street executives displayed. They had long since abandoned any sense of truth in their pro-

THE TOP 1 PERCENT OF THE TOP 1 PERCENT, AS THE OCCUPY MOVEMENT WOULD DESCRIBE THEM, HAD NEARLY DESTROYED THE WORLD'S FINANCIAL SYSTEMS.

SIMPLY STATED, TRUTH MATTERS.

fessional lives and any sense of responsibility to say no to an endless stream of financial instruments that were devoid of value but filled with the potential of fast and big profits. This was a classic "bubble" where objectivity was lost in a sea of irrationality and exuberance. The bubble was slowly depressurized by a series of massive federal bailouts and capital infusions. The carnage on the Street, and streets, and in the lives of millions of individuals was difficult to measure. All of it was unnecessary. The top 1 percent of the top 1 percent, as the Occupy movement would describe them, had nearly destroyed the world's financial systems.

Simply stated, truth matters.

* * * * * * *

Now that we've taken a brief look at some of the historical and philosophical developments of truth and its role in our lives, how are we to think about this in today's world? First, each of us has to decide if we are to conform reality, or truth, to ourselves, or are we going to conform *ourselves* to our best understanding of reality/truth? I propose to you that it is very difficult if not impossible to build a coherent life if we are regularly changing the basis upon which we attempt to live. Human beings long for secure footing they can navigate from as they journey through their lives. It is very difficult to make powerful and meaningful movements without the leverage that comes from a strong foundation.

To illustrate this, think about scenes from the movie *Gravity*. If you haven't seen this 2011 flick, starring Sandra Bullock and George Clooney, it's worth picking up. In short, Bullock and Clooney, astronauts, are completely free, untethered, and without restraint in space. In other words, they are, in one very real sense, completely *free*. And this in a state that is not restricted by gravity or any other restraining force. At the same time, as troubles mount with conditions in space all around them, they are powerless to act in a meaningful way. In this sense, being totally *free* will result in death unless they (the astronauts) are acted upon by some outside force. It is the same with us. A life that possesses no reference points from which to live has no secure footing from which to gain leverage and power for its journey. Is that really how we want to live?

My proposition is that there is absolute and unchanging truth that serves as a critical reference point from which we can live. I have named these reference points *unchanging points of light* as a metaphor for ancient navigation. Have you ever been at sea or in the countryside on a pitch-black night? If you have, you know how disorienting it feels as all of your landmarks and reference points are not visible. What is left to you to navigate with is the night sky and the celestial objects that are illuminated. Those stellar reference points are absolute and unchanging, or at least changing in very precise and predictable patterns. In fact, the changes are so precise that, with today's technology, we can go to any date in history and any geographic location on earth and reproduce the night's sky. Amazingly but predictably ordered!

Human beings long for that amazingly predictable order. In my view, the most clear and present danger to each individual, our nation, our culture, and our world is that we seem to live in darkness. Our ability to critically think about our lives, our nation, our culture, and our world is diminished, disoriented, and distorted—we have sprinted away from a foundation of truth. It is as if the facts lay before us, but the filter of our assumptions, ideology, and belief systems are so thick that reality can't get in.

Isaiah was a Hebrew prophet who lived and wrote between 700 and 600 B.C. In describing the state of Israel in his day, Isaiah also described today's Western culture—precisely. He wrote, in Isaiah chapter 1, verses 5-7:

Where will you be stricken again? The whole head is sickened; the whole heart is faint. From the sole of your foot even to the head there is nothing sound in it, only bruises, welts, and raw wounds, not pressed out or bandaged, nor softened with oil. Your land is desolate, your cities are burned with fire, your fields . . . strangers are devouring them in your presence. It is desolation, as overthrown by strangers.[3]

Wow! Isaiah nailed it for our modern world. Strangers are devouring our fields in front of our eyes, and we can't see it. The darkness is killing us.

The proponents of a postmodern world are advocating an expansion of true freedom through the removal of what they would say is "the illusion" of truth, the morality that accompanies truth, and its restraint on our lives. That choice is a choice for darkness, not enlightenment. Historically, the abandonment of truth has led to some form of anarchy. The resulting lawlessness always leads to a loss of freedom. An objective look at any people-group, nation, or culture that has suffered through periods of anarchy will reveal misery, suffering, injustice, and chaos of immense proportion. In that environment, individuals will feel powerless about their lives. Again, the movie *Gravity*: you see a perfect example of human beings who are totally unrestricted by anything while at the same time powerless to make any meaningful movements. If these astronauts do not find some point of reference to gain power or leverage from, they die. It

IT IS THAT SIMPLE WITH US AS WELL; IT IS JUST NOT AS IMMEDIATELY OBVIOUS. THIS IS JUST LIKE THE PEOPLE ISAIAH WROTE ABOUT. THEY COULDN'T SEE IN THE DARK THAT WAS RIGHT BEFORE THEIR EYES.

is that simple. It is that simple with us as well; it is just not as immediately obvious. This is just like the people Isaiah wrote about. They couldn't see in the dark that was right before their eyes.

We have been given so much by so many at such a great price. It seems that today we value life, freedom, opportunity, justice, and the dignity of each individual human being so little that we are willing to throw it all away in some kind of postmodern meltdown. But it doesn't have to be this way. Someone—perhaps *you*—will step up, take a stand, and pay the price.

* * * * * * *

As I wrote this chapter, the world was still mourning the senseless killing of innocents in multiple premeditated terrorist attacks in Paris and San Bernardino, California. With the unyielding chaos and conflict in our world, it is so easy to just give up and give in to the forces of evil and corruption that relentlessly impose their will on the rest of us.

I know you don't run a nation, an army, and likely do not possess a great deal of international influence. What you do have is the power of one. I was reminded of the power of one last week in a visit to the Dallas Holocaust Museum. The power of one crazed ideologist to take over a great nation and nearly conquer the free world with all the evil that accompanied his untested and grotesque view is extremely disturbing. The museum is designed to have that kind of effect on its visitors. The life of Anne Frank and others like her, at the same time, is incredibly inspiring while visiting this museum. Both types of people are reminders that, today, innocent people all over the world are being slaughtered by modern-day perpetrators of evil ideologies and the practices that result from those ideologies.

You can be a person who rejects ideology and insists on

the pursuit of truth in all aspects of life. You can examine all the assumptions you have made in your life and demand of yourself those assumptions that reflect the most current understanding of reality that is possible. This will require you to experience the tension that occurs when you examine the evidence around you every moment of every day and then contrast that evidence with what you currently believe. Great achievement almost always demands this type of great tension.

If you are willing, then perhaps, one person at a time, we might find our way out of darkness and into a more enlightened world. This is my hope as we continue our journey in this book.

ONE TAKEAWAY FROM THIS CHAPTER

Most of the Western world believes truth is moldable, flexible, and adaptable to the map of the world individuals have created in their own minds. What do you say? Is there anything so precious and powerful that you believe it to be an unchanging point of light worthy of defending and preserving for both present and future generations?

TWO

LIFE

"The magic of the mechanisms inside each genetic structure saying exactly where that nerve cell should go— the complexity of these mathematical models is beyond human comprehension."[1]

—ALEXANDER TSIARAS, MATHEMATICIAN AND AUTHOR

My contention with this book is that everything is built on truth. From there, we have common standards for the important discussions in life.

Like the idea of *life* itself.

It is the one thing upon which so many other things depend. Our view of the value of human life, our understanding of the origin of life and what constitutes the beginning of life, determines many of the most critical views that exist.

Where does life begin? How do we define it?

To begin with, we need to define life *biologically*. Then we need to define it *philosophically* and *legally*. To many, the subject of life seems as though it is well established and agreed upon. It is anything but.

Life is generally defined as the ability of an organism to metabolize energy (consume and process food) and reproduce. In mammals, most people would equate a heartbeat and brain activity as a measure of life. And they do. However, the known complexity of life demands a better definition. So it seems that science, medicine, and law continue to look for these answers in the minutiae of a living cell.

After an unprecedented amount of work, science found what it was looking for.

On June 26, 2000, President Bill Clinton stood on the White House steps with Dr. Francis Collins to announce the completion of the Human Genome Project that Dr. Collins had led. It was, perhaps, the greatest scientific achievement of the last century. In Clinton's remarks, he said: "Without a doubt, this is the most important, most wondrous map ever produced by humankind. . . . More than one thousand researchers across six nations have revealed nearly all 3 billion letters of our miraculous genetic code. I congratulate all of you on this stunning and humbling achievement. Today, we are learning the language in which God created life. We are gaining ever more awe for the complexity, the beauty, the wonder of God's most divine and sacred gift."[2] Ever the great orator, President Clinton said it much better than I ever could.

> "TODAY, WE ARE LEARNING THE LANGUAGE IN WHICH GOD CREATED LIFE. WE ARE GAINING EVER MORE AWE FOR THE COMPLEXITY, THE BEAUTY, THE WONDER OF GOD'S MOST DIVINE AND SACRED GIFT."

Now, fifteen years later, what is the impact of this accomplishment on our lives and culture? To begin with, federal, state, and municipal law view DNA as the most complete, specific, and unique definition of human life. Not just that a sample of DNA represents a human life—but that it identifies *which* human life, to a remarkable degree of accuracy, from the billions of possibilities that exist! This is so much so that people are convicted of or exonerated of crimes based solely on DNA analysis.

In medicine, DNA plays a remarkable role in the diagnosis and treatment of many physical conditions. It identifies genetic traits and tendencies. It can also establish the racial and geographic history of an individual.

All this begs a question. When is a person's unique complement of DNA established? Much science tells us it is completely established by the time of the first cell division after fertilization. As you know, a baby is a unique combination of both of its parents' genetic traits. At the same time, its DNA is distinctly unique and different from either parent! The DNA is essentially a complete set of instructions and part of the vehicle to produce every protein required to express every trait the baby will have. Yet, at any point of development as a fetus, infant, toddler, child, adolescent, or teenager, the unique life that has been created represents an incomplete expression of its DNA. Perhaps the expression is only complete at the end of life, as some conditions are not apparent until later in adulthood.

As foundational as DNA is, it only represents one part of the enormous complexity of human life. A cell is the basic structural, functional, and biological unit of all known living organisms. Generally, cells are considered the building blocks of life as they are the smallest units of life that can replicate independently. They consist of cytoplasm enclosed in a membrane that acts as a barrier and filter. Each cell contains many different types of biomolecules, including enzymes, DNA, RNA, and many other proteins. Necessary to the function and health of each individual cell are energy systems, protein synthesis systems, reproductive systems, information systems, and the intricate interactions between all these systems. The efficiency of all of these processes working together is extraordinary.

To multiply all of that, each human being contains more than ten trillion cells! Paul Davies, author of *The Fifth Miracle: The Search for the Origin and Meaning of Life*, says this: "Each cell is packed with tiny structures that might have come straight from an engineer's manual. Minuscule tweezers, scissors, pumps, motors, levers, valves, pipes, chains, and even vehicles abound. . . . The various components fit together to form a smoothly functioning whole, like an elaborate factory production line. . . . At the level of individual atoms, life is anarchy-blundering chaos. Yet somehow, collectively, the unthinking atoms get it together and perform the dance of life with exquisite precision."[3] Wow! I only wish I could have said it so well. At the risk of offering an additional thought to the statements of a highly credentialed and accomplished quantum physicist, I suspect that the "blundering chaos" Dr. Davies spoke of, at the atomic and subatomic levels, is actually highly ordered complexity that is just currently beyond our ability to observe and measure with contemporary technology. So it just appears chaotic rather than ordered. In any case, the efficiency of a cell is staggering. That efficiency requires enormously ordered functioning systems that interact with one another at a level and in ways that

I SUSPECT THAT THE "BLUNDERING CHAOS" DR. DAVIES SPOKE OF, AT THE ATOMIC AND SUBATOMIC LEVELS, IS ACTUALLY HIGHLY ORDERED COMPLEXITY THAT IS JUST CURRENTLY BEYOND OUR ABILITY TO OBSERVE AND MEASURE WITH CONTEMPORARY TECHNOLOGY.

are simply beyond human description.

This is not a book on cell biology; there are plenty of those already written. What I am attempting to do is to invite you to look at the details. It is in the details where we can really get our eyes open to the unimaginable complexity, efficiency, interdependency, and intentionality of life at the most fundamental level. It inspires wonder and awe in anyone who looks. It was meant to.

So how are we to think about the beginning of life on this planet? The answer to that question determines how one views everything else. History has proven that. Ancient people associated almost every aspect of life with divinity or a specific divine being. Admittedly, they invented these gods in the legends and mythology of each culture and people-group. Regardless, ancient people associated life with a divine source. As formal religions developed, in differing ways each one attributed life to a supernatural state, supernatural beings, multiple gods, or a singular omnipotent creator-God.

That would hold true until the modern era of Western thought. This era became a combination of philosophy, science, and literature. For the first time in all of history, modernists proposed that life began as a series of random, small sequential events taking place over hundreds of millions of years—events completely explainable by natural uncaused events. This theory required no supernatural intelligence, influence, or direction. It also carried with it a profound loss of meaning that is associated with the intentional creation of life by a Creator-God who has the position, power, and authority to declare the value and purpose of each individual life.

The difference between those two positions represents the profound conflict that exists and has existed for well more than one hundred years on the issue of the origin—and value—of human life on our planet. Again, prior to this modern revolution, God was the author of life, the sustainer of life, the provider and protector of life. After the revolution, man was the determiner of life through science, technology, and enlightenment. The revolution of modernism represented the convergence of many ideas.

* * * * * * *

First, there was a scientific revolution that came from, of course, Charles Darwin.

On November 25, 1859, Charles Darwin published his seminal book, *On the Origin of Species by Means of Natural Selection, or the Preservation of Favoured Races in the Struggle for Life*. (This is the full and original title, though it is most commonly known as "On the Origin of Species.") Darwin's idea of natural selection was intended to explain how the most complex of life forms, human beings, began as simple life forms that evolved. In other words, all life forms evolved from one original, simple being through small sequential changes across hundreds of millions of years. Darwin's ideas were very elegant and profound. They changed how we think about life. But his ideas also require a functioning life system in order to have the capacity to begin and continue the process of change. So there was a gap. A huge gap. Under the theory, planet Earth began as a random collection of organic and inorganic molecules. In order to begin the development of life, the random molecules had to become highly ordered self-replicating molecules that led to highly ordered biochemical systems that led to the very first cell. In their ex-

As INTOXICATING AS THE IDEA IS, IT JUST DOESN'T STAND UP TO SCIENTIFIC AND MATHEMATICAL STANDARDS. IT LACKS THE ESSENTIAL POWER TO EXPLAIN HOW RANDOM CHEMICALS BECAME SELF-REPLICATING.

uberance of scientific discovery and modern philosophical thought, Darwinian evolutionists extended his theory backward in an effort to bridge those enormous gaps.

As intoxicating as the idea is, it just doesn't stand up to scientific and mathematical standards. It lacks the essential power to explain how random chemicals became self-replicating. I don't know of any idea that adequately explains the enormous leap from lifeless random collections of matter to the ordered complexity, intentionality, and energy that describes the most simple life forms. But those very obvious and basic problems have not stopped Darwinian evolutionists from trying to bridge the enormous gap. They hold out for the discovery of a mechanism that will "jump-start" the process. Once life actually begins, evolutionary theory becomes possible; some would say probable. There is evidence to support this idea. And there is evidence that doesn't.

A great deal of hope for the Darwinian believers came from the Miller-Urey experiments at the University of Chicago in the 1950s. The scientists passed electrical currents though an experimental atmosphere of gases and chemicals that were thought to likely have been present in early earth. The results included some amino acids, the building blocks of proteins.[4] Unfortunately, the atmosphere that they used was later established to not be a possibility, and the results could not be reproduced with what was believed to be the most likely gas composition of an early earth atmosphere. Still, their ideas lived on.

Many theoretical and applied mathematicians have attempted to make calculations of the probabilities of establishing certain conditions that are necessary for life. One such calculation was completed by Sir Fredrick Hoyle and his colleague, Dr. Chundra Wickramasinghe, in the 1970s. They determined that there are approximately three thousand enzymes necessary for proper cell function.[5] The mathematical probability of those enzymes forming as a random natural event are somewhere in the neighborhood of one chance in ten to the *40,000th*-power. As a point of reference, the number of atoms estimated to exist in the known universe is less than ten to the 100th-power. Amazingly, that is just the enzymes! We still have to account for the DNA and all the other essential components of a cell. When other calculations have been attempted, the results have been the same. *The creation of the most basic molecules required for life from random uncaused events is a mathematical impossibility.* And this has led to other ideas to explain the origin of life on earth.

Hoyle and others have proposed the *pan spermia theory.* It says that there is a great deal of organic debris in space and that some of it was transported to earth by a meteorite or other cosmic objects. However, even if that happened, it would not change the essential problem of the mathematical probability of producing precise, complex, and self-replicating molecules required for life from random processes. It just changes the origin of this organic matter and actually adds improbability as the life forms would have had to survive the transportation to and impact with earth!

Another idea says that the first life forms came from deep sea vents. This is a very interesting idea, but it possesses the same problem; it merely changes the proposed location and environment. The environment may be improved, but the math is the same. The idea is a no-go. In other words, to build a case for the origin of life beginning as a random, uncaused

THE IDEA IS A NO-GO. IN OTHER WORDS, TO BUILD A CASE FOR THE ORIGIN OF LIFE BEGINNING AS A RANDOM, UNCAUSED NATURAL EVENT REQUIRES A MECHANISM THAT IS YET TO BE DISCOVERED.

natural event requires a mechanism that is yet to be discovered. At the same time, Darwinian evolutionists demand that any explanation be limited to natural law, scientific standards, and methodology, without a causing agent acting on the elements present on earth prior to life. Those demands and the evidence available to us are at odds with one another. The longer Darwinian evolutionists wait for the missing mechanism, the more difficult their problem becomes.

So the science of life is developed to extraordinary levels. The questions and disagreements exist around what to do with the science. We routinely expect that all but the most dire of medical conditions are, predictably, treatable. Many of my elderly patients tell me we are keeping people alive too long just because we can. Dr. Atul Gawande, a general surgeon in Boston, thoroughly documented several extremely complex medical cases in his book *The Checklist Manifesto*.[6] Gawande's conclusion was that what is possible in modern medical therapeutics has exceeded human capacity to manage. In other words, there are so many different therapies in place at the same time that the medical community can't manage them all without overlooking some of the basics.

* * * * * * *

The arguments over the biological basis of life and the origin of life lead us to a stark fundamental and philosophical conflict. The conflict is based in the assumptions that we make about life, *random and uncaused* versus *intentional and caused*. There are many voices in our culture that point to a completely random, uncaused beginning of life. One such voice in academia is Dr. Peter Singer. He is the Ira DeCamp professor of bioethics at Princeton University. Singer is well known for his work in animal rights and humanitarian efforts to alleviate hunger and other forms of human suffering. He is one of the most credentialed, accomplished, and recognized bioethicists in the world. In an interview on a Dallas radio station in 2012, Dr. Singer said: "In the West, the value of human life was established in Genesis 1."[7] He was referring to Genesis 1:26, where the Bible says: "Let us make man in our own image, according to our likeness." Being the image-bearers of God, in other words, means that each individual human life is sacred and of immeasurable value regardless of race, status, or righteousness—if this is one's belief and life philosophy.

However, Dr. Singer went on to say he did not believe what was written in Genesis and rejected the idea of a Creator-God. In that interview, he said that he believes men and women are simply animals evolved to a higher level. Therefore, their value is perhaps marginally greater than animals, but not dramatically so. Once one holds that position, life is no longer sacred and does not possess an inherently robust value—there is no Creator-God with the authority and power to declare it so. What is one left with? There is just the opinion of man. That opinion varies dramatically because of ideology, culture, and morality. In some cultures members believe you are to love your neighbor. In other cultures, they believe you are to eat your neighbor! Of course, each culture has its own practices and beliefs that vary greatly.

History has given us great and noble acts that come from the love of one person for the other and the enormous value of life that fuels those noble sacrifices. But more often than not, a look at history reveals the opposite. Man's inhumanity to man has wrecked hundreds of millions of lives. There appears to be no limit to the creativity and length that man will go to in his expression of his own ideology, self-interests, and struggle for power, wealth, and fame.

A look at one of those great cultures, Rome, is instructive. Ancient Rome was a great empire that conquered and ruled much of the known world. Its accomplishments and contributions to our world still stand as a testimony to what is possible. But Rome fell from a meltdown of ethics, morality, and sound living. A thirst for indulgence, power, greed, corruption, and sex of all kinds dominated life. A high value of life cannot co-exist with that kind of culture as violations of human dignity and life itself are routine and required to perpetuate such an environment.

Within that mess, the lives of children are most at risk; they are always the most vulnerable. How a culture treats the lives of children is a primary determinant of the health, stability, and future of that culture. Abortion, infanticide, and child abandonment were common practices in Roman culture. Children were not viewed as a sacred gift. Rather, they were viewed as being undesirable, even burdens. Many of the pagan cultures routinely practiced child sacrifices to their pagan gods. These were horrific acts of death by fire or scalding heat in a red-hot crucible. These practices were part of why God ordered the destruction and death of entire communities in the Old Testament. From the time of these ancient cultures until today, human beings have been bought and sold for slave labor, sex, and pretty much anything slave owners or those in dominance of those lives want. It goes without saying that no sense of human dignity exists within these kinds of practices.

Human dignity was missing in the horrors of communist Romania under Nicolae Ceausescu. In my first visit to that county, in 1999, ten years after the dictator's death, the streets of Braila, Romania were gray and without life, still. The average person on the street would not make eye contact with me. When they did, there was no life in their eyes.

Then I met the people of Holy Trinity Baptist Church, and their pastor, Joseph Stefanuti. I saw life and hope in these people like I had never seen before—anywhere. It was truly amazing. The difference? They overcame the persecution and indignities of their day-to-day lives with the transformation that is given by the author of life. I could *feel* the difference; it was palpable.

Let's leap forward to the effects of modernism on the subject of life. Modernism was grounded in the ideas that education, technology, and social reordering would lead to a better world and society. It was the convergence of new scientific ideas from Darwin and others, new social reordering from Marx and others, and killing the idea of God in our lives and culture via the work of Nietzsche and others. We have already looked at the impact of Darwin, so let's take a brief look at how the ideas of Nietzsche and Marx impacted the value of life.

Frederick Nietzsche was a brilliant thinker, writer, and philosopher. Nietzsche was the son of a minister. Both of his grandfathers were ministers. So, unlike most of the critics of the Bible and Christianity, Nietzsche was well educated in Scripture, theology, and doctrine. He had a better understanding than most of what he was rejecting. According to what he wrote, Nietzsche's experiences of the horrors of war caused him to reject the idea that there could be an omnipotent, caring God who would allow such carnage and loss of life to happen. Many agree with his conclusions. But Nietzsche also knew that killing the idea of God in culture would have consequences. He said the loss of the restraint of God would lead to the bloodiest century in all of history. And he was right.

Nietzsche also wrote of something he called The Final Man. Yet, he seemed to write about that idea with great disdain. His complaint focused on the delusion that men would have in thinking they had a moral basis for good without a source of goodness, God. Again, he predicted—and with precision—

the modern dilemma. Man searches for good in a world that is absent of the source of righteousness, justice, and goodness. In that self-deterministic world, man has and will make decisions about life that fit his desires of the moment, his current understanding and perspective of life, and his limited ability to understand the consequences of his decisions.

HIS COMPLAINT FOCUSED ON THE DELUSION THAT MEN WOULD HAVE IN THINKING THEY HAD A MORAL BASIS FOR GOOD WITHOUT A SOURCE OF GOODNESS, GOD. AGAIN, HE PREDICTED—AND WITH PRECISION—THE MODERN DILEMMA.

As Marx's ideas were implemented, they merely transferred power from the aristocracy to a new ruling elite class. The Marxist order carried with it the power to determine who lived and who didn't. It also determined *how* each person lived. It determined the rules for how many babies each family could have or should have. It determined where people live and who they work for. This was true from the urbanization and population policies in China to the reordering of Romania under Ceausescu in the 1970s and '80s. The value of life became what *the state* determined it to be. The consequences to human life were horrific.

In contrast stands the one thing that can make all other things insignificant in comparison. It is the declaration by a holy God that men and women are created in His image. As such, the only being with the power, authority, and position to grant immeasurable worth and dignity to each individual life did so out of the limitless abundance of His love and position as author and creator of all life.

At first, this might seem like a very ordinary thing; we in

the West have become somewhat accustomed to the idea. But on closer examination, it becomes obvious that every effort of man to establish the identity of individual human beings fails to deliver the goods. All major religions and belief systems attempt this. Hinduism establishes a class of people that are essentially without value and dignity. See the movie *Slumdog Millionaire*. Islam sacrifices the value of the individual to the importance of the whole system of belief, culture, law, and government. Buddhism does not establish a belief or connection to a transcendent and personal creator-God. Instead, it relies upon individual human performance and effort. The Buddha's last words were "Never cease striving." That statement sounds noble—and on some levels, is—but it is also an exhausting way to live. The Buddha himself struggled to eliminate desire from his life as he pursued a life of the most extreme deprivation possible, stopping just short of death. He realized it was essentially not humanly possible to eliminate all desire, so he pursued different remedies for the maladies of mankind as he saw them. Marx believed that the individual would change and improve how he lived when the economic system he lived in changed. Neither happened. Instead, Marx's ideas created a head-on collision leading to man's inhumanity to man.

A few years ago I had the pleasure of visiting Bangalore, India. I loved the people I met and worked with. There are many cultural differences between India and the United States. The most difficult for me was the contrast between extreme wealth and extreme poverty that I found existing side by side. Often, there is only a wall separating a slum from a mansion. The marginalization of the lowest class of people is just a way of life. Essentially, I found no hope for anything different. In fact, I did not even observe any tension in the culture to change it.

The most vivid example came in the form of a missionary whose full-time service was collecting people on the streets who were dying. He operated a warehouse with beds where he would bandage wounds and give these people a place to live until they passed away. I don't have words to describe the indignities these people suffered.

We began this chapter with my statement that life is the one thing on which so many others depend. If we believe that life is a precious gift, accompanied by purpose and meaning, that is granted by our Creator as we were made in His invaluable image, then our positions are essentially established. Those positions state that the dignity and value of each person are determined by their Creator and not by their position in culture, nor by their striving. The complexity of a living cell inspires wonder and awe; it is truly divine. The most sophisticated algorithms created by man are woefully inadequate to describe the massive cascade of complex biological events that occur from the conception of human life to its birth and subsequent development. To state it another way, there are no mathematical formulas, verbal descriptions, or scientific principles to adequately and thoroughly explain the energy, information, and intentions required to produce human life or, for that matter, any form of life. It is divine.

In my view, all of this demands that we view and treat human life, in fact *all life*, with great respect and worth. And it begs a very simple question: "Is the baby growing in its mother's uterus a human life?" If it is not, then who has the right to tell a woman what she must do? If it is, then who has the right to take an innocent human life?

* * * * * * *

To my friends, family, and colleagues who are reading these ideas on life and have had, or supported, an abortion in the past, my heart goes out to you for the very difficult and overwhelming decision you had to make. I might have made the same decision at certain points in my life. There is not now, nor will there ever be, judgment in my soul regarding the decision you made. I will simply hope and pray that you have healed from the pain.

Since 1973 in the United States of America, where the founding documents establish that each human being is endowed by his or her Creator with certain inalienable rights—among them "Life, Liberty, and the Pursuit of Happiness"—that same America has ended more than sixty million lives of babies with a distinct, unique, and complete complement of DNA.

Science, medicine, and the law state that DNA is the definition of life. What do you say? More importantly, what will you do with that?

MEDICAL TESTIMONY

Science gives us a marketplace in which to examine the details of life in the most objective manner possible. This allows all sides to engage in a constructive debate. Science is not held captive by one ideology or another. It is intended to be held captive by the data.

In that sense, to end this chapter, I have organized references and quotes from several medical experts and textbooks to serve as a resource. The evidence is broad-based and compelling.

Let's begin with expert medical testimony.

In 1981, a United States Senate judiciary subcommittee received the following testimony from a collection of medical experts (the Subcommittee on Separation of Powers to Senate Judiciary Committee S-158, Report, 97th Congress, 1st Session, 1981):

"After fertilization has taken place a new human being has come into being. [It] is no longer a matter of taste or opinion. . . . It is plain experimental evidence. Each individual has a

very neat beginning, at conception."
—Dr. Jerome LeJeune, professor of genetics,
University of Descartes

"By all the criteria of modern molecular biology, life is present from the moment of conception."
—Professor Hymie Gordon, Mayo Clinic

"The beginning of a single human life is, from a biological point of view, a simple and straightforward matter—the beginning is conception."
—Dr. Watson A. Bowes, University of Colorado
Medical School

"It is incorrect to say that biological data cannot be decisive. . . . It is scientifically correct to say that an individual human life begins at conception."
—Professor Micheline Matthews-Roth,
Harvard University Medical School

The official Senate report reached this conclusion:

Physicians, biologists, and other scientists agree that conception marks the beginning of the life of a human being—a being that is alive and a member of the human species. There is overwhelming agreement on this point in countless medical, biological, and scientific writings.[i]

* * * * * * *

Advocates of abortion have made compelling public statements regarding the essence of what abortion actually does.

Faye Wattleton, the longest reigning president of the largest abortion provider in the United States, Planned Parenthood, argued as far back as 1997 that everyone knows that abortion kills. She said, in an interview with *Ms.* magazine:

> *"I think we have deluded ourselves into believing that people don't know that abortion is killing. So any pretense that abortion is not killing is a signal of our ambivalence, a signal that we cannot say, 'Yes, it kills a fetus.'"*[xi]

Naomi Wolf, a prominent feminist author and abortion supporter, made a similar concession when she wrote in *The New Republic:*

> *"Clinging to a rhetoric about abortion in which there is no life and no death, we entangle our beliefs in a series of self-delusions, fibs, and evasions. And we risk becoming precisely what our critics charge us with being: callous, selfish, and casually destructive men and women who share a cheapened view of human life. . . . We need to contextualize the fight to defend abortion rights within a moral framework that admits that the death of a fetus is a real death."*[xii]

Peter Singer, contemporary philosopher and public abortion advocate, joins the chorus in his book *Practical Ethics:*

> *"It is possible to give 'human being' a precise meaning. We can use it as equivalent to 'member of the species Homo sapiens.' Whether a being is a member of a given species is something that can be determined scientifically, by an examination of the nature of the chromosomes in the cells of living organisms. In this sense there is no doubt that from the first moments of its existence an embryo conceived from human sperm and egg is a human being."*[xiv]

Bernard Nathanson cofounded one of the most influential abortion advocacy groups in the world (NARAL) and once served as medical director for the largest abortion clinic in America. In 1974 he wrote an article for the *New England Journal of Medicine.* Keep in mind the article was written in the immediate shadow of Roe vs. Wade. Nathanson wrote:

"There is no longer serious doubt in my mind that human life exists within the womb from the very onset of pregnancy."[v]

Some years later, Nathanson would reiterate his views.

"There is simply no doubt that even the early embryo is a human being. All its genetic coding and all its features are indisputably human. As to being, there is no doubt that it exists, is alive, is self-directed, and is not the same being as the mother—and is therefore a unified whole."[vi]

Other sources of medical science include:

"Biologically speaking, human development begins at fertilization."
—"The Biology of Prenatal Develpment," *National Geographic*, 2006.

"The two cells gradually and gracefully become one. This is the moment of conception, when an individual's unique set of DNA is created, a human signature that never existed before and will never be repeated."
—"In the Womb," *National Geographic*, 2005.

* * * * * * *

Textbooks

"Human development begins at fertilization, the process during which a male gamete or sperm unites with a female gamete or oocyte to form a single cell called a zygote. This highly specialized, totipotent cell marked the beginning of each of us as a unique individual."

"A zygote is the beginning of a new human being."
—Keith L. Moore, *The Developing Human: Clinically*

Oriented Embryology, 7th edition (Philadelphia: Saunders, 2003), pp. 16, 2.

"Development begins with fertilization, the process by which the male gamete, the sperm, and the female gamete, the oocyte, unite to give rise to a zygote."
— T.W. Sadler, *Langman's Medical Embryology,* 10th edition (Philadelphia: Lippincott Williams & Wilkins, 2006), p. 11.

"[The zygote], formed by the union of an oocyte and a sperm, is the beginning of a new human being."
— Keith L. Moore, *Before We Are Born: Essentials of Embryology,* 7th edition (Philadelphia: Saunders, 2008), p. 2.

"Although life is a continuous process, fertilization (which, incidentally, is not a 'moment') is a critical landmark because, under ordinary circumstances, a new genetically distinct human organism is formed when the chromosomes of the male and female pronuclei blend in the oocyte."
— Ronan O'Rahilly and Fabiola Müller, *Human Embryology and Teratology,* 3rd edition (New York: Wiley-Liss, 2001), p. 8.

"It is the penetration of the ovum by a spermatozoan and resultant mingling of the nuclear material each brings to the union that constitutes the culmination of the process of fertilization and marks the initiation of the life of a new individual."
— Clark Edward Corliss, *Patten's Human Embryology: Elements of Clinical Development* (New York: McGraw Hill, 1976), p. 30.

A quote from the Abort73 website powerfully describes the state of abortion in 2017:

"In America today, there is only one group of human beings for which being human is not enough: 'unwanted,' unborn children. The inconvenience of their existence has resulted in a legal loophole of shameful proportions. They're small. We can't see them. They're in the way, so we define personhood in a way that conveniently excludes them. How is that tolerant and inclusive? If it is morally reprehensible to kill a developing human being after birth, it is no less reprehensible to kill a developing human being before birth."

—http://abort73.com/abortion/personhood
(accessed November 28, 2016)

* * * * * * *

A Final Word

The attitudes, beliefs, policies, and laws of the citizens, policy makers, and elected officials of the United States regarding the lives of unborn babies has resulted in the intentional death of more than sixty million human beings. Medical science and a parade of medical expert witnesses have established that conception represents the beginning of human life.

Are we willing to continue to ignore established science and pretend that the practice of abortion on demand is ethically and morally acceptable and consistent with our Constitution, which declares a right to life for each and every human being?

You have the power of one to influence the final outcome of this debate.

References

i. Report: Subcommittee on Separation of Powers to Senate Judiciary Committee S-158, 97th Congress, 1st Session, 1981, 7.

ii. Faye Wattleton, "Speaking Frankly," *Ms.*, May/June 1997, Vol. VII, Number 6, 67.

iii. Naomi Wolf, "Our Bodies, Our Souls," *The New Republic,*

October 16, 1995, 26.

iv. Peter Singer, *Practical Ethics,* 2nd ed. (Cambridge: Cambridge University Press, 1993, 2008), 85, 86.

v. Bernard N. Nathanson, M.D., "Deeper into Abortion," *New England Journal of Medicine,* November 28, 1974, Vol. 291, No. 22: 1189-1190.

vi. Bernard N. Nathanson, M.D., *The Hand of God* (Washington, D.C.: Regnery Publishing, 1996), 131.

ONE TAKEAWAY FROM THIS CHAPTER

There have long been common misperceptions about the science of life, the value and dignity of life, and the origin of life. The truth of these issues is critical to your understanding of the rest of life.

My challenge is to dig deeper into these questions of life to find truth. Do this in the way that works best for you: study, read, journal, pray. Doing so will make all the difference.

THREE

LOVE

"(Love) . . . bears all things, believes all things, hopes all things, endures all things. Love never fails."

—1 Corinthians 13:7, 8

We are witnessing—no, experiencing—one of the greatest frauds of all time. It is saturated in our conversations, both public and private. It defines political correctness as that term is defined for us these days. Violating this precept is to define yourself as the lowest of the low of humanity. Yet it has no power to transform the hearts of men and women where the problem really lives. It is the quintessential example of contemporary men and women substituting their own solution for truth . . . when truth just seems too old-fashioned or even irrelevant.

What is this fraud? "Tolerance." It has a relentless companion: "diversity." These two concepts are eroding the truth, damaging relationships, and polarizing society further and further into groups that demonize one another and exist in perpetual conflict. The more that culture demands "tolerance," the more intolerant we become.

Tolerance is grounded in the idea that there is something *to* tolerate in someone, which means that one group has the power and authority to judge another. It doesn't. It is grounded in the negative, that there are comparative deficiencies . . . one person to another . . . one group to another. In fact, we are all deficient in one way or another. Tolerance has its basis in our pride . . . that we are better . . . know better . . . do better than the next person. That pride leads us to the conclusion that we are all inherently good by nature. The historical evidence of mankind tells a different story. It is a story of the tension between the good and evil that lives in us all.

History reveals an illustration of man's inhumanity to man. It also reveals a story of men and women sacrificially giving themselves away for the good of others. So, in that basis of being right ourselves—*doing* right ourselves—we are required to tolerate others who are different than ourselves. Even in my words, you see a lot of the use of "self."

Clearly in all of this, the focus is on self, rather than a focus *above, beyond*, and *outside* of oneself. We need a focus on something—Someone—greater than ourselves to gain an accurate perspective of our very being. Really, all of this describes the tension that exists between what is really good in all of us and what is not. So, if being trained in "diversity" and being directed to "tolerate" others was going to work, it would have. Instead, the ideas have been, and are, abject failures as evidenced by the growing conflict and tension that exists between the many different groups that make up our nation and world.

The idea for this chapter came to me more than two years ago. As I have written (and rewritten) it, the world, our nation, my state, and the city I live in have witnessed one tragic event after another. In just the last thirty days since my writing of this chapter, a radical Islamic terrorist murdered forty-nine innocent people in a nightclub in Orlando. Another radical Islamic terrorist murdered eighty-four people in Nice, France simply by driving his truck down a crowded boulevard. An attempted coup in Turkey against the prime minister, who had fundamental Islamic views and affiliations, left more that 160 dead. Two African-American men in different states were killed by police in what appeared to be an unnecessary use of deadly force. In response to that, a man in Dallas shot and killed five police officers and wounded seven more in a rage of revenge over the two police shootings. To heighten the tragedy, the police officers were shot as they were attempting to keep a peaceful protest of those two shootings a safe event for anyone to attend. It turned out to be life-threatening for the peacekeepers. By all accounts from the police officers and protestors, there had been friendly, supportive, and productive interactions between the police and protestors.

In addition to these violent examples, the murder rate in Chicago, a great American city, is unprecedented and shows no signs of abating; police have stopped engaging potential criminal behavior that they observe on the streets. The murder rates in many of our cities are, by definition, more than we should accept. It is madness. It is tragic. It violates every standard of human decency. It is also an indictment of our growing lack of understanding of one another and the absolute explosion of anger, conflict, and frustration between people who look different, believe different, perhaps behave different, think different, and come from different nations and socioeconomic people-groups. Given all of that and the many more examples of conflict I could provide, why would we think that more than fifty years of diversity training and tolerance imperatives would be effective strategies and tactics to unite diverse people-groups?

I celebrate and support freedom, opportunity, and inclusion for all people. I believe we should identify all barriers and engage in an aggressive and relentless war to tear down barriers to freedom, opportunity, and inclusion for all people, but especially for the marginalized and disenfranchised.

Unfortunately, often those barriers live in the strongholds of our hearts and minds. Changing them seems nearly impossible. Not changing them is the equivalent to surrendering to all the darkness that accompanies these strongholds.

* * * * * * *

The July-August 2016 edition of *Harvard Business Review* focused on diversity in the workplace. In the first of three articles on diversity, Frank Dobbin and Alexandra Kalev, both Harvard professors of sociology, tackled the question of "Why Diversity Programs Fail." They wrote: "It shouldn't be surprising that most diversity programs aren't increasing diversity. Despite a few new bells and whistles, courtesy of big data, companies are often doubling down on the same approaches they have used since the 1960s, which often make things worse and not better. Firms have long relied on diversity training to reduce bias on the job, for hiring tests, and for performance ratings in recruitment and promotions and grievance systems to give employees a way to challenge managers. These tools are designed to preempt lawsuits by policing managers' thoughts and actions. Yet laboratory studies show this kind of force feeding can activate bias rather than stamping it out. As social scientists have found, people often rebel against rules

UNFORTUNATELY, OFTEN THOSE BARRIERS LIVE IN THE STRONGHOLDS OF OUR HEARTS AND MINDS. CHANGING THEM SEEMS NEARLY IMPOSSIBLE. NOT CHANGING THEM IS THE EQUIVALENT TO SURRENDERING TO ALL THE DARKNESS THAT ACCOMPANIES THESE STRONGHOLDS.

to assert their autonomy. Try to coerce me to do X, Y, or Z, and I'll do the opposite just to prove I am my own person."[1] These two sociologists share more: "Executives prefer a classic command and control approach to diversity training because it boils down expected behavior to do's and don'ts that are easy to understand and defend. Yet this approach flies in the face of nearly everything we know about how to motivate people to make changes. Decades of social science research point to a simple truth: You won't get managers on board by blaming and shaming them with rules and reeducation."[2] In addition, they write: "It turns out that while people are easily taught to respond correctly to a questionnaire about bias, they soon forget the right answers. The positive effects of diversity training rarely last beyond a day or two, and a number of studies suggest that they can activate bias or start a backlash. Nonetheless, nearly half of the midsized companies use it, as do nearly all the Fortune 500 [firms]."[3]

In the subsequent article, Iris Bohnet writes: "Diversity training programs largely don't change attitudes, let alone behavior."She goes on to reference the work of John Dovidio and colleagues at Yale. They evaluated the effects of anti-bias training on first- and second-graders in sixty-one classrooms. About half the classrooms were randomly assigned to get four weeks of sessions on gender, race, and body type with the goal of making the children more accepting of others who were different from them. The other half didn't receive the training. The program had virtually no impact on the children's willingness to share or play with others. She went on to say, "This doesn't mean that you can't ever teach kids to be more accepting—just that improving people's inclination to be inclusive can be incredibly hard." Finally, she makes a most important point: "For beliefs to change, people's experiences have to change first." [4]

Dobbin and Kalev vividly demonstrate this in a World War II story: "At that time, the U.S. army was still segregated, and only whites served in combat roles. High casualty rates left general Dwight Eisenhower understaffed, and he asked for black volunteers for combat duty. When Harvard sociologist Samuel Stouffer, on leave at the War Department, surveyed troops on their racial attitudes, he found that whites whose companies had been joined by black platoons showed dramatically lower racial animus and greater willingness to work alongside blacks than those whose companies remained segregated. Stouffer concluded that whites fighting alongside blacks came to see them as soldiers like themselves first and foremost. The key, for Stouffer, was that whites and blacks had to be working toward a common goal as equals—hundreds of years of close contact during and after slavery hadn't dampened bias."[5] I wonder if Stouffer studied the effects on the black soldier? I would speculate he would have found the same result. The results of Stouffer's survey should surprise nobody. They did not surprise me.

SO WHAT IS THE ANSWER TO THE DILEMMAS OF BIAS, BARRIERS, AND BAD BEHAVIOR?

So what is the answer to the dilemmas of bias, barriers, and bad behavior?

The answer, in my view, has been the subject of most poets, songwriters, and storytellers for all of time. It is love, pure and simple. But it is not just any kind of love. Rather, it is the kind of love that every human being longs for in the part of himself or herself that feels the deepest and hopes the most. It is that kind of unconditional love that endures all things. The kind of love that is able to look past all the differences and disagreements to see what is really present inside someone. A kind of love that is grounded in the inherent worth and dignity of each person regardless of how different they are from us. A love that we are only capable of extending because it has been extended to us. This kind of love is transformational in our very being—a game-changer, if you will. The power it unleashes in us is like no other force on earth. "Tolerance" holds no power to change our hearts. However, love has the power to accomplish anything. Enough power to accomplish what seems impossible. I have witnessed it. So have you. From Shakespeare to the Bible. "Love never fails" is the famous quote—even to the nonreligious—from 1 Corinthians 13. Think about this: where does love begin? In human relationships. It begins with accepting the other person right where they are, just as they are. It requires you and me to set aside everything else and just do that singular thing. It does not mean that you agree with, approve of, or endorse the life of the other person. It does not mean that accepting them will be easy—but it does mean that it is necessary.

Love is grounded in another belief as well: We are all much more alike than we are different. When it comes down to it, each person has similar and deeply felt human needs, including unconditional acceptance, unconditional love, significance, and an experience of competence at the essential tasks of life. These are true regardless of how radically different we might appear. Unfortunately, we also share something else: human failure, pain, and suffering. I have not met the person who is immune to failure, pain, and suffering; these are universal experiences. The significance, I believe, is that human failure, pain, and suffering connects our hearts regardless of our differences. It is the fuel that drives our engine of empathy and what really lets us know we are all very much alike. It is what happens if we take the risk to walk in someone else's shoes for a few miles and experience the injustice that they live with. That they suffer from the conflict in their lives. That we share their disappointment of betrayal. That we walk in the tension that exists because we know the right thing to do and find ourselves doing something else. Those few examples give us a sample of the difference love makes when it propels us into someone else's inner world. Love is the fuel that powers us to take those steps.

A focus on "diversity," in contrast, produces exactly what you would expect the word to do: divide. It has been the focus of social and cultural retraining for decades. It is intended to foster understanding and respect in the melting pot of people we call the United States. And in the day and age of a very flat world, it is intended to help us engage all kinds of people-groups. Yet, the movement has intentionally drawn attention to the differences between each of us. It has been wildly successful in doing so! In fact, by directing all of our attention to our differences, we have forgotten what we have in common. Now we live, act, and govern in constant conflict and gridlock from every polarized position possible. Every different group, race, and belief system is acutely aware of how much it disagrees with the other, and therefore each group just digs in further. It is as if we hold no value of unity. It seems we believe we can succeed as a nation and culture by moving in countless different directions at the same time. In all of history, can you point to any nation divided that has enjoyed success? I can't, and you also will have a hard time doing so.

> IN FACT, BY DIRECTING ALL OF OUR ATTENTION TO OUR DIFFERENCES, WE HAVE FORGOTTEN WHAT WE HAVE IN COMMON.

So how are we going to bring unity from diversity? Interestingly, the word *university* comes from this combination: unity from diversity. But the true answer for all of us is found in the idea of truth (chapter 1 of this book). A university contains many different disciplines, philosophies, backgrounds, ages, educational trainings, and perhaps even great geographical differences. However, a healthy and thriving academic culture is both driven by and accountable to a pursuit of truth in all things. Even if it is a painful pursuit! It does not determine the answers in advance through ideology, it seeks the answers through rigorous and objective academic work. This sounds much easier than it is in reality; it requires that we separate human beings from deeply engrained beliefs that do not always hold up to investigation.

The key here is that if two people possess radically different views, yet are both yielded to peer-reviewed published research literature as a truth source, they share a commonality that can produce a productive dialogue. In some cases it can even lead open-minded people to work together on projects and research that were in the areas of their disagreement. Being accountable to something greater than ourselves has great power to unite human beings. Love, then, is like the glue that holds people together. The ultimate unifying force is when human diversity finds unity in its pursuit of deity.

The public concept of tolerance has simply brought us more intolerance. Diversity has brought us more division. The words themselves suggest that. The antidote to all of this is love. It begins one person at a time. It was expressed beautifully by Dr. Jerry Root of Wheaton College in a chapel service to seniors on April 27, 2007:

"See in others what is really present in them. Don't miss what they might be doing and how they might be living, and how we might, in seeing them, extend to them what we have received [unconditional acceptance, eternal significance, abundant love]."

When love is your operating system, then someone's possibilities become much more clear. You see what is truly present and not so much what is missing, damaged, or different. Love focuses our hearts and minds on our commonality . . . and it possesses enormous power to unite us.

If love could be limited to one type of expression—and it certainly can't—I believe it would be best illustrated in the devotion that one person gives to another, especially when the person receiving is incapable of loving back. I witnessed this very thing in the life of my uncle, George Elliott.

George was one of the most interesting people I have ever known. He was born in 1923 in Belgium; he was a teenager when World War II began. During that time he participated in the Belgium resistance, guiding people to one part of the country or the other. After the Allied troops liberated Belgium, he served in the newly formed army. He completed college, earned a degree in finance, and then began a career as a diplomat. It was while serving as the Belgian consulate to Houston that he met and married my Aunt Hay, in 1968. They lived all over the world and then settled into a quiet retirement in Texas. Hay contracted Alzheimer's and began the steady decline that is so evident in that life-stealing disease. During this time, as she became increasingly confined to her bed, George spent all day, every day, by her side. Day after day, week after week, month after month, year after year he was there—all day, every day. That is an impossible task unless every ounce of your being loves that person. It is the fully human expression of "love never fails."

DAY AFTER DAY, WEEK AFTER WEEK, MONTH AFTER MONTH, YEAR AFTER YEAR HE WAS THERE—ALL DAY, EVERY DAY. THAT IS AN IMPOSSIBLE TASK UNLESS EVERY OUNCE OF YOUR BEING LOVES THAT PERSON.

I have pondered the many different ways I could illustrate what I mean by love—unconditional love. Repeatedly, the words and life of my pastor, Buddy Liles, came to me.

It was one of the most horrifically vivid scenes of 2015. Twenty-two Egyptian Coptic Christian men working in Libya were marched out to a beach and beheaded. They were given the option of refuting their faith in order to live. They declined.

One by one for the entire world to see, these men were mercilessly and gruesomely beheaded, being guilty only of dissent from the radical Islamist ideology of ISIS. Every ounce of me wanted to execute a slow, painful, and torture-filled death for the perpetrators of this mass execution as well as for their leaders who ordered it. In fact, I personally wanted to impose the punishment on them.

Then, it happened. I showed up at church. Buddy starts to teach. With a full projection of the images now familiar to all, the photo of the morbid beach scene behind him, Buddy says:

"We need to pray for these ISIS soldiers. In spite of our anger and desire for revenge, we need to remember that Paul persecuted, arrested, tortured, and murdered Christians prior to his conversion on the road to Damascus. God in his infinite wisdom chose to transform Paul and use him in extraordinary ways to build his kingdom. There may be a Paul among these ISIS executioners."

I didn't see that coming. It hit me hard. As always, Buddy was spot-on in his remarks. The idea of praying for men who are the living and breathing definition of evil is counter to every instinct and response I have, and yet it is exactly the response of God to mankind, especially given their rejection of Him. It is also what we are commanded to do if we are going to follow Him. It is a burden, if you will. It is also a clue to the *meaning* of unconditional love. That is a kind of love that loves when everything about you doesn't want to . . . doesn't feel like it . . . when we are essentially incapable of generating that feeling. It is an intentionality that is beyond thinking, feeling, or objectivity. No wonder every human being longs for this genuine acceptance.

I cannot conceive a bigger divide than that existing between myself and those ISIS executioners. The only—and I mean only—force in the universe that could possibly close the gap between me and them is love. Do you think you can educate me into understanding them? Do you think you can demand that I be tolerant of them because of their economic, cultural, governmental, or religious upbringing that brought them to this kind of behavior? No, you can't. Neither can you for almost every person that you know. You will only increase the gap between us. You will build more anger and resentment as you try. Such an attempt is not just destined to fail. It is destined to make things worse.

And that is essentially what all of the efforts at diversity training and tolerance have done. That is one of the main reasons we live in increasingly polarized, conflicted, and contentious groups. It is just another way to violate the truth about human beings and human behavior.

> IT MUST BE A RESPONSE THAT IS BEYOND US. IT MUST BE A FULL-TILT, ALL-CONSUMING EXPLOSION OF GRACE. IT MUST BE THE GIFT OF ALL GIFTS.

Every human being seeks unconditional acceptance. But it is an acceptance that is grounded in love, powered by love, and directed by love. It is not a love that has its source in us. It is a love that must be sourced *from* something . . . from *someone* greater than ourselves. It must be a response that is beyond us. It must be a full-tilt, all-consuming explosion of grace. It must be the gift of all gifts. It must forever consume us and leave us as new creations capable of new things. Then it will have the power to change the hearts of men and women, which is exactly where the problem lives in the first place. That includes my heart. As always, my heart is a work in progress. I'll bet that yours is as well. My heart has been wounded so many times in so many ways that I have lost count. Unfortunately, many of the wounds were self-inflicted.

If the concept of love as foundational in all of life resonates with us, then we will have much more in common than we previously thought. It hits us where we love one another: in our hearts. Once we can accept someone, then we are capable of building a relationship grounded in respect of one another, even in the midst of profound disagreement. Love powers us through the very natural and expected tension that we feel when we meet someone who is radically different from ourselves. It also gives us a reason to build a relationship with someone that we would not or could not otherwise build. A relationship with someone from a different nation, belief system, sexual orientation, socioeconomic level, age, or many other things that might divide us.

In my view, all of this begins and ends with the value of each human being. In the Western world, our view of the value of human life is established in Genesis, as God revealed through Moses: we were made by God, in His image, for His purposes. I agree with Dr. Singer (see previous chapter) on this point! That view of an omnipotent, omniscient, and eternal holy God who is responsible for all that we are and all that is compels each of us into a view that a right relationship with other human beings is to be grounded in love—imitating the love that he showed us. It may be best expressed here:

Love is patient, love is kind, it does not envy, it does not boast, it is not proud. It is not rude, it is not self-seeking, it is not easily angered, it keeps no record of wrongs. Love does not delight in evil, but rejoices with the truth. It always protects, always trusts, always hopes, always preserves. Love never fails.

1 CORINTHIANS 13:4-8

"Love never fails" is the most powerful force in all the universe, in all of time, and in any and all circumstances.

Many think this is all just ideological pie-in-the-sky fluff. A Darwinian evolutionist holds to the idea of the modernists and postmodernists, claiming we human beings are random collections of molecules with no inherent meaning to our lives. They would say that all of the human experiences of love, devotion to one another in relationships, the need for justice, the need for meaning and morality, the desire to understand our origins and our destinies—these are all just incremental evolutionary developments that increase our ability to survive.

But let's think about such thinking. Can you honestly reduce all of your human experience to biochemistry? Call every psychiatrist in your town and ask them how their patients will be doing if they are told they have no sense of purpose and meaning inherent in their lives.

Think about this scenario. In a very romantic and emotion-packed moment, you want to express yourself to the love of your life. In your own words and in your own way, you tell that person how much you love them. You experience their response and begin to grow closer and more connected. Now, in a secular, Darwinian, evolutionary kind of way, try telling the love of your life that you are experiencing a "biochemical moment" about them—and then see what kind of response you get. You might be lucky to leave without a life-threatening injury! And yet that is what we are asked to believe. All human experience can't be reduced to mere biochemical events. There is much more to being human.

I can establish this very point—scientifically—in the development of newborn babies. What I mean is that we can observe and measure the development of and well-being of brand new lives as they unfold before our eyes. There is great science unfolding today about the effect of the mother and others around the mother during pregnancy; it is amazing material to study. One thing that has long been developed is the need within a baby to be nurtured by its mother or someone who is substituting for the child's mother. This nurturing can't be explained by biochemistry or survival in evolutionary ideology.

I have personally witnessed what happens when this connection is missing. In multiple trips to Romania, I have observed firsthand the problem of so many orphans in that nation. I have also witnessed babies in institutional nurseries who are provided food, shelter, and other basics, but who receive no human nurturing. Some of them fail to thrive and die. Some of them live, but are so detached from human interaction that they are destined for profoundly disoriented and dysfunctional lives. In either case, it is profound evidence that human beings are much more than biology. Perhaps it is evidence that the power of love impacts the most fundamental part of our core—the will and ability to live.

> PERHAPS IT IS EVIDENCE THAT THE POWER OF LOVE IMPACTS THE MOST FUNDAMENTAL PART OF OUR CORE—THE WILL AND ABILITY TO LIVE.

* * * * * * *

My experiences in Romania surprised me. First, I made great friends with our partners at the church. They were full of life, full of joy, and full of hope in the midst of any and all circumstances. I got to know people on the other side of the world who spoke a different language, grew up in a different nation, and experienced a profoundly different culture from myself. And yet I discovered that we were much more alike than we were different. I discovered so many things that I admired, respected, and enjoyed in my new friends. It was transformational.

What my pastor, Buddy, challenges us to do year after year is what he calls "neighboring." He means: reach out to people in your neighborhood that you don't know. Invite them into your home for dinner. Invite them into your life. Ask them about theirs. You'll discover commonality and find yourself more understanding, and perhaps you will find out that you are really more alike than different.

What would happen if each of us decided to reach out to someone who we might enjoy, but someone very different from ourselves? We could begin to share meals together and maybe other life experiences in which we would come to know more about one another. We would learn of each other's hopes and dreams, trials and tribulations, successes and failures, and maybe even crack open the brokenness in each of our hearts. Would that help us understand one another? Would that motivate us to pursue different solutions to our problems? It would. It would tear down many barriers that unnecessarily exist. It would shine a very bright light on what is the same about all of us and, in so doing, soften our hearts and build bridges between us.

In the end, the worst person that you know and the best person that you know are just trying to find their way through this very dark world. The worst person that you know has probably surrendered their life to evil and various destructive elements in the world. The best person that you know is running hard after the best things that this world and its creator have to offer. *But neither of those two extremes are beyond transformation.*

His instrument was and is love. The best thinkers and writers I have ever known call that kind of love: *amazing.* It has the power to carry you through and past the abyss.

God, our Creator, loves us in a way that is beyond human comprehension. He gave us all that He has to give. His instrument was and is love. The best thinkers and writers I have ever known call that kind of love: *amazing*. It has the power to carry you through and past the abyss.

You be the judge: tolerance versus love. Which holds the power to transform the world around you? More importantly, which holds the power to transform the world inside you?

ONE TAKEAWAY FROM THIS CHAPTER

Find a way to share a meal this week with someone completely different from yourself/your family. They may come from a different country, different belief system, or different socioeconomic group. Ask thoughtful questions about their lives, hopes, and dreams, as well as their problems. Share yours with them. I promise it will be impacting, and none of you will be the same.

FOUR

IDENTITY

"Well it may be the devil or it may be the Lord,
But you're gonna have to serve somebody."[1]
—BOB DYLAN

What does it mean to be *you*? That is a question each person answers for herself or himself, regardless of their intentions or awareness. How are we to think about our identity in a postmodern world where reality is described as an illusion? When there is no such thing as truth? Under this thinking, there is only truth and reality as they appear to you.

I realize a college classroom seems the more appropriate place for such philosophical questions. However, the students in those classrooms eventually leave. They enter the practical world of work, raising families, and community involvement. But with those graduates, at least in part, come some of the ideas of the classroom. Give those students a few decades of personal ascent into cultural, business, and community leadership positions, and the opportunity for those ideas to develop, and you have a living, breathing revolution of thought.

On the surface, such an ideological revolution may seem to

have many desirable qualities. Deep below that surface, however, where our identity is formed and lives, we are searching for something to hang onto. In our contemporary world, that something is moving, constantly changing, slippery. That something does not possess the power we need to navigate through this world and establish secure, stable, and meaningful lives. To establish that kind of life, our identity needs to be developed and grounded in that which is truly and eternally powerful. But increasingly, we place our identities in that which does not provide life or is not foundational to life, and the result is something woefully inadequate to provide for our needs.

Let's venture into the messiness and brokenness, as well as the possibilities, in our lives. I promise you this can be a journey in pursuit of hope. I believe hope is what fuels all of our lives, regardless of our beliefs.

* * * * * * *

One of the greatest thinkers and writers of all time was Leo Tolstoy. In the 1870s, around the age of 50, Tolstoy went through a profound moral crisis followed by an equally profound spiritual awakening. In describing his identity crisis, he said: "As long as we are intoxicated by life, everything is OK. But when we sober up . . . " Among other things, Tolstoy was sobered by his experiences in the

AMONG OTHER THINGS, TOLSTOY WAS SOBERED BY HIS EXPERIENCES IN THE CRIMEAN WAR. IT WAS AT ABOUT THIS POINT, HE SAID, THAT LIFE TOOK HIM TO THE EDGE OF THE ABYSS. EVENTUALLY, EACH OF US WILL JOIN TOLSTOY IN SOME KIND OF PAINFUL, SOBERING EXPERIENCE.

Crimean War. It was at about this point, he said, that life took him to the edge of the abyss. Eventually, each of us will join Tolstoy in some kind of painful, sobering experience. A serious medical diagnosis, the horrors of war, the loss of a loved one, a financial reversal, betrayal by a trusted friend, or, if by some miraculous sequence of events we are shielded from all of these, then facing the end of life is guaranteed to seriously sober each of us. Some of us know these painful life events all too well. Some of us do not. The question is: are we prepared?

The answer, in my view, will be found in how well our identity is established and in what it rests. Is our identity powerful enough to carry us through and past the abyss? If you lost everything in your life—your health, family, friends, career, and wealth—then what would remain of *you*? Is it enough? Could you stare into the abyss and live? Not just exist, but *really* live? These questions are difficult, but at the same time they are some of the most important questions we will ever ask. They are worth our time, our best effort, and whatever it takes to discover the answers.

Our identity is generally thought to be the conception of one's self, what makes each of us unique. The formation of our identity occurs through each of our unique identifications and interactions with significant others, beginning with our parents and siblings. We will aspire to some characteristics, values, and beliefs that we experience with them, or we may reject what we see, feel, and experience with those we're closest to early in life. Our identity can be charted in a series of stages formed in response to increasingly sophisticated challenges as we grow. These challenges revolve around explorations, experiences, and commitments that we make. We will move toward that which is most attractive to us. So it seems to me that our identity has its beginnings outside of our choices and in our family of origin and those closest to our family. And in the same way, we have a physiological and emotional connection with our mother and the people closest to her during her pregnancy. Their voices and their emotions impact us.

Infants and toddlers live in a world that is determined by their parents and, to a lesser degree, others. Their parents hold the power to love, share affection, nurture, teach, interact, and discipline their children. They have the same power to withhold, limit, or manipulate these qualities. The differences are dramatic. The first child will have a foundation of significance, competence, and inclusion. The second child will have a void he or she is likely to spend a lifetime trying to fill. The development of their identities will come from two entirely different places with two entirely different burdens.

As we journey through our young lives in elementary school, we begin to view ourselves in certain ways that expand beyond our family. Often, it is the way in which we get most rewarded or most criticized. An attractive girl begins to identify with her beauty. A boy that excels in sports views himself in terms of his athletic performance. An intelligent boy or girl views himself or herself through their intellect and academic achievement. The class clown rises and falls by how well he or she makes people laugh. The people-pleaser is rewarded by how well he accomplishes satisfying others. When the most dominant qualities in the eyes of others is lacking, real or imagined, then the opposite type of identification develops. And this development can lead to extremely insecure, even dark, places.

I heard one of the most poignant stories that illustrates this well for me in a series of workshops I attended in my training as a dentist. The dentist teaching our workshops is one of the best dental practitioners I have ever known, and he is an equally fabulous teacher. This man, Frank, told us of a patient who came to him to redo veneers (a thin layer of material over teeth to improve looks or provide strength) that had just been completed. There was nothing wrong with the veneers, but the patient thought they were too yellow. My dental teacher redid them, he told us, using the lightest porcelain shade available. Afterward, she returned, complaining that they were still too yellow. Frank handed her a porcelain shade guide with every shade and asked her to pick the one that appeared to be the color of her teeth. She selected a very colorful yellow shade. On Frank's instruction, she held it to her teeth and looked in the mirror. She quickly saw her perception had been way off. She turned to Frank and said—regarding how she saw herself—"This is my problem, isn't it?" He responded by asking her when she began to believe she had yellow teeth. In second grade, she said, one of her classmates told her she had yellow teeth and began to tease her. It is entirely possible that her teeth were a very normal color!

Kids can be brutal. Identities are delicate. If something that small can cause someone to carry around an identity that alters the reality of what is plainly in front of them in the mirror—and do so for decades—then what can something extremely significant do to how we identify and view ourselves?

As we move into high school, the complexity of our challenges grow. In a hyper-connected world, the popular boys and girls live and die—too often literally—by their social performance. Or things as insignificant as a wrong Tweet or a liked Instagram post. Making the right friend in middle school can introduce one to incredibly fun, healthy, socially connected peers who are thriving, and to their families, which are also likely doing well. These relationships can determine an entire middle school and high school experience. The absence of them can propel a teen into much different kinds of relationships, ones that have the power to be self-limiting or even destructive. Everyone has distinct memories of middle school and high school experiences. Some of those memories are satisfying and filled with abundance. Others are filled with disappointment. All impact our identity in very powerful ways for years to come. In these vulnerable and developing years, the question is: can we . . . can *anyone* . . . build enough substance to provide a meaningful life foundation?

Next comes college or some type of life pursuit away from home. At this stage we begin to take on many of the qualities, skills, concepts, and views built into us, and there begins to form a sort of grand experiment—a personal stew of beliefs about ourselves, others, and the world around us. Again, this has been developed by family, friends, peers, culture and, yes, media of all kinds. Today's youth—and all of us—are saturated in a nonstop stream of media messages and continuous connections. With it, the positive foundations of family and relationships and their influence on us take a serious hit. Perhaps even a fatal hit.

In this new stage of life, we take on new authority figures and new influences from numerous sources. Yes, they can easily replace our family's influence, at least for a period of time. These include college professors, new friends, new communities, new responsibilities, expanded experiences, and new ideas that, hopefully, we put through rigorous tests in this newly discovered marketplace. This all works best if that marketplace is a "free market" in which dissent and individual thought are valued, encouraged, and viewed as healthy. Often, that is not the case.

This period of transition into independent adult life is supposed to establish what our unique view of the world is and speak to how we fit into that world. Maybe some of these larger perspective changes come at our first full-time job.

They usually challenge what came before them. They will also expose our deepest desires and the gaps, pain, and depth of our universal needs.

The transition into independent adult life can be a slow burn or an explosion of identity expansion. We begin to form an answer to the question, "What is the most attractive me, to me, that I can become?" In today's world we are self-deterministic-addicted machines. People in our modern-day Western culture seek total control in determining who they are, how they live, and their roles in life. This includes biology, sexuality, relationships, family structure, career, business, education, governmental policies, faith, and all the consequences involved in the disrupting of our long-standing cultural standards and norms.

> WE BEGIN TO FORM AN ANSWER TO THE QUESTION, "WHAT IS THE MOST ATTRACTIVE ME, TO ME, THAT I CAN BECOME?"

From that foundation—the converging lines of influence, and our deterministic desires—an identity begins to take form. If beauty, intelligence, athletic ability, achievement, career, status, sports, music, or art occupy the bull's-eye of that which is most attractive to us, then that is what we will look for to define ourselves. The more we feed that beast, the more it grows within us. All the endless choices the world presents to us are distractions from that which is really foundational; they are inadequate, exhausting, and in the end, empty.

Let's take a brief look at some examples. First, the beauty queen. When your whole life revolves around beauty, fashion, and competition with your peers, the obvious fleeting nature of beauty, the pain of living up to impossible standards, and this highly competitive dogfight reveal themselves for what they are: pathways to disappointment and loss. I am not demeaning the value of beauty or pageant competition. Many women have built great lives and careers with that platform. They had the extraordinary benefit of beauty grounded in substance. But beauty, the competitive nature of beauty, fashion, and sex make for an incredibly unstable identity.

How about the athlete? I used to enjoy playing in a charity golf tournament benefiting Athletes In Action, the Christian organization focused on serving professional athletes. I know at least part of what you are thinking (because I think it too!): professional athletes make millions of dollars and enjoy every possible benefit of celebrity status. But they also experience some unique problems and pains. Think about this for a minute. From elementary school through college, highly sought-after athletes exert extraordinary amounts of time on athletic and sports development and training. They might become the "superstar athlete," which seems an enviable position for any guy, but it also comes with consequences.

John Weber, the director of Athletes In Action in Dallas, said his most challenging work begins when a professional athlete retires. In an instant, all the stardom is gone. The on-field achievements . . . the locker room relationships . . . the competition . . . the superstar status . . . even the *purpose* for each day . . . disappears, and there is little to take its place. Unless deliberately and intentionally, often painstakingly, a bigger and stronger purpose has been developed in the midst of a professional athletic life. According to John, a wonderful family is often the most essential ingredient to helping a retired athlete transition to a new phase of life. However, by itself, even that is often not enough. The pain can run deep.

Then take the clothing, cars, and cash state of mind. To many of us, we have a style of dress, appearance, and lifestyle that fits us. We don't make that much of these things; they are just what they are. For others, style, brand, look, the club, the car, the status—they are everything. When we have to have those things to be OK, we've placed our *identity* in those things, and our very well-being is threatened. We'll even take huge or entirely unnecessary risks to achieve the status we believe we need. This state of mind is absolute confirmation that our life revolves around our material identity.

Finally, and perhaps in great contrast to the previous examples, let's look at a modern-day example with tragic consequences. This person represents the convergence of multiple cultural and technological developments. He is the mass shooter.

This type of criminal profiles mainly as young, angry, ideologically extreme, carrying a distorted and sometimes indulged view of reality, and being isolated in small groups of like-minded individuals connected by the Internet. When a person has normal social interactions with others, their distortions in thinking get challenged and often modified into a more healthy state. When one becomes isolated socially and connects mainly with a very small number of like-minded individuals who are geographically separated but united, online, in a cause or mind-set, those contacts reinforce the distorted thinking. This rebellious identity grows so strong that some of the individuals actually act on their acquired convictions. Yes, they are disturbed. They are also a product of many forces.

One of those forces is violence in the media. In 2015 Harvard University completed a systematic review of the effect of violence in the media on violent behavior. This review of peer review-published research spanned thirty years and three thousand articles; it was a massive undertaking. It represents the absolute highest level of research available on the topic today. The researchers, to no one's surprise, concluded that violence in the media has a direct tie with increased violent behavior.

And yet so many Americans produce, promote, and play killing video games all day, every day. Games that have no real consequence or tie to actual death. It is killing without the consequence of killing. A hunter knows that when you hunt and shoot a bird, you see, feel, and experience a dead animal. Whether you agree or disagree with hunting, the distinction is critical.

Movies are no better. We get exquisitely designed audio/video graphic violence. It may be futuristic. It may depict current life situations. But all of it desensitizes us to the potential consequences of violence—injury, pain, and death. War is a real and sometimes necessary experience needed to defeat evil. It is also horrific and has horrific consequences on living, breathing, emoting human beings. Movies, video games, and television shows attempt to sanitize war; they can't. What they can do is contribute to destructive thinking and behavior.

> MOVIES, VIDEO GAMES, AND TELEVISION SHOWS ATTEMPT TO SANITIZE WAR; THEY CAN'T. WHAT THEY CAN DO IS CONTRIBUTE TO DESTRUCTIVE THINKING AND BEHAVIOR.

All of this converges in a perfect storm that allows an individual to take on an imagined identity in a twisted world he or she has created. Given enough opportunity and lack of accountability, this person can become the next mass shooter; tragedy awaits.

Identities are powerful. They drive behavior. They are the fabric of our lives. They are worth our best effort and highest consideration.

Let me offer some hope from a real-life story. Tiffany is a teller at a branch of my bank in a suburb of Dallas/Fort Worth. One day last summer, I had a stack of transactions I needed help with. Tiffany was fun, bright, helpful, good at her job, and expressive. As I got to know her, we talked about raising kids, the complexities of the world, and various other ideas. After a few minutes of discussion—I was impressed with her intellect—I told her I wanted her to run for president of the United States. We both agreed she would be a better choice than the two candidates—Hillary Clinton and Donald Trump— we had in 2016 national election. She went on to tell me she was raised by her grandparents and that her grandfather was a very strict man. He would walk her onto the school bus every day until she was in the eleventh grade; this provided a great deal of embarrassment. She had strict curfews and many other mechanisms in place to protect her, and these things, at the time, mostly annoyed her.

I asked her how she viewed them now. She said those protections, that love, provided the foundation for her life. It sounded to me like her grandfather believed Tiffany was extremely precious and worth protecting at all costs. *What is that worth?* When the most important authority figure on earth to this little girl—now a wife and mother—lives in such a way that his life is dedicated to protecting her, building her, and viewing her as precious, well, what kind of identity would that build in her heart and mind? It is an extraordinary, abundant identity. It is an unchanging point of light.

IT SOUNDED TO ME LIKE HER GRANDFATHER BELIEVED TIFFANY WAS EXTREMELY PRECIOUS AND WORTH PROTECTING AT ALL COSTS. *WHAT IS THAT WORTH?*

* * * * * * *

So the pattern of our identity goes something like this. We start as a blank canvas and, literally, our unique DNA begins to paint colors on that canvas. Those colors can be intense or subtle. They can be blended or separate. Our parents' makeup shapes them into more distinct images, and these develop into a living, breathing, dynamic composition. After birth: more painting takes place on our canvas. Others in our family and close inner circle begin to add still more to these distinct characteristics. Sometimes the additions are intentional, sometimes they are not.

Then each of us gets to pick up the brush and paint still greater detail about our lives. We will likely refine our painting over the years, many times. The questions become: What have I surrounded myself with? What have I immersed myself in? What most attracts me? What has answered my deepest and biggest questions? What *moves* me? What has seemingly satisfied my perceived needs? Those answers are all part of the image we paint of ourselves. We can only paint a picture of the images that we see, feel, or experience. It is why the attractions, surroundings, immersions, motivations, and satisfactions of our life experiences are so essential in defining what it means to be you or me. The possibilities are endless. The obvious question is: are they big enough, powerful enough, and true enough for an abundant life, one in which you move in the direction of your highest calling and live out what was intended and possible for you?

The world presents exciting, seductive, and powerful images that can intoxicate us. But remember the words of Tolstoy: "When we sober up . . . " Life is wonderful and painful at the same time. We live in the tension between those two poles. The wonderful is not guaranteed. The painful is. Our identity is the vehicle that drives us through all of these experiences. So, how about you? Is your identity prepared to endure and survive the battles in front of you? Will it carry you past the abyss?

And then there is the speed of life, which keeps us from slowing down long enough to examine ourselves at any level of depth. There just isn't the time to do so as we rush from one place to another, answering texts and emails or posting on Facebook, Twitter, and Instagram. We are reading six different blogs, doing yoga at 5:30 AM before work, and we keep putting off that class at our local community college, the one that would enhance our skill sets. It can be near madness. So, slowly, gradually, unnoticeably, we grow a mile wide and an inch deep. We can turn around an email with three different attachments at nearly the speed of light, but when we most need it, facing the abyss, our emotional and spiritual bank accounts are empty.

This is not an intellectual dumbing down, it is a dumbing down of our *souls*. Absent energy and devoid of well-developed substance for our souls, we reach for antidepressants at an alarming rate; we visit our physician way too often and way too young, possibly because degenerative disease or an early form of cancer has already visited us. We attempt to escape by immersing ourselves in whatever satisfies our particular desires. That satisfaction is rarely healthy or truly satisfying. It often merely intensifies our pain.

> WE ATTEMPT TO ESCAPE BY IMMERSING OURSELVES IN WHATEVER SATISFIES OUR PARTICULAR DESIRES. THAT SATISFACTION IS RARELY HEALTHY OR TRULY SATISFYING. IT OFTEN MERELY INTENSIFIES OUR PAIN.

Almost every people-group ever studied has found a way, has made a priority of, worship. Modern people are no different. However, as Western culture has marginalized faith and religious expression in a relentless pursuit of secularism, the objects of worship have taken on a more worldly form. That form is defined by the current thinking of the culture and what attracts the minds, hearts, and lusts of men and women. People turn to sheer idolatry. Take even a quick look at *People* magazine, *Entertainment Tonight*, or the endless stream of

Internet accounts on entertainment and sports celebrities. Why do we follow their lives, listen to their opinions, and measure our lives relative to, say, those of a mega-wealthy celebrity? It is simple. They have become modern-day idols. We fool ourselves into believing we should value what they value.

There is an old English word for that which holds ultimate value. It is to *hallow*. I tried to find a modern word for its substitute. I couldn't. When I looked up the definition of hallow, I found its origin in the old English word *halgain*, defined as "to make holy or to honor as holy." Holy is generally associated with divinity, and it often carries the meaning of being "set apart." The part of us that desires a relationship with the divine, to *engage* with the divine, is the part of us intended to be truly foundational. It is the part where we feel so deeply that it hurts. Identity is intended to rest in the most essential and foundational aspect of each of us.

Once more, let's reference Genesis 1:26. The author, perhaps Moses, recorded that God declared: "Let us make man in our own image according to our likeness." The extraordinary value of each of human being is established by the only Being with the position, power, and authority to declare it so. The author of life, God is also the sustainer of life and provider of life; we are meant to look to Him for life. That includes how we define ourselves, the meaning of our life, and what we call morality. It includes the perspective of where we came from . . . and where we are going.

That's an identity that will provide a true, and unchanging, point of light.[2]

ONE TAKEAWAY FROM THIS CHAPTER

How do you identify yourself? Another way of asking this is with two questions: "If you lost everything in your life, what would remain?" And, "Would it be enough to sustain you?"

Answering these questions truthfully can be the first step toward a new identity that is powerful enough to sustain you through any abyss. Take the time to do this; your future is worth it.

FIVE

RACE

*"I have a dream that my four little children will one day
live in a nation where they will not be judged by the color of
their skin, but by the content of their character."*
—Rev. Martin Luther King Jr., August 28, 1963

Slavery is and was barbaric, inhuman, immoral, and profoundly destructive. It is a dark stain on the fabric of the United States of America. It was and is based in lies. Of all of the nations on earth, America should have known better. Our very Constitution declares that the sovereignty, worth, and dignity of each individual human being is established by our Creator. And yet this country bought into the lies that were popular, and leaders and landowners justified them with the most twisted and distorted thinking. Instead of resting in the declaration of a holy and almighty God, we relied on the ideas of men.

Ideas have consequences. The economic, pseudo-scientific, and anthropological arguments in support of slavery were as unfounded and incorrect as human arguments could be, and yet America persisted. How was that possible? The answer,

AMERICA PERSISTED. HOW WAS THAT POSSIBLE? THE ANSWER, SADLY AND TRAGICALLY, LIES IN THE HEARTS OF MEN AND WOMEN. SO DOES THE SOLUTION.

sadly and tragically, lies in the hearts of men and women. So does the solution.

To be fair, throughout all of history, one group or another, in one way or another, has been marginalized and victimized by those with power and influence. This is not a problem limited to recent history. It is a problem for all of history. Having said that, I want to focus on the more modern era of slavery that encompasses the last three hundred years.

Modern thought, with its roots in the ideas of Immanuel Kant, really got a kick start from Charles Darwin. Developing a theory on the origin of life without the need for a Creator-God changed the world's perspective, then and now. The full title of Darwin's seminal book comes as a surprise to many: *On the Origin of Species by Natural Selection or the Preservation of Favoured Races in the Struggle For Life*. The natural selection part is widely expected. The "favored races" part is often missed or overlooked. The questions become: which races are favored? Who decides? The answers came from the intellectual elite of the day. Mostly, they were European Caucasian men. It's easy to guess which race received the favored treatment.

I am mostly descended from European Caucasians. I have American Indian and Hebrew ancestry as well. So I am the typical American citizen with several racial compositions. I have enjoyed learning about that part of myself and my family. It makes for a great story to tell of my grandmother's sisters in small-town Texas, otherwise fine women who thought they had been Baptist since the time of Moses, only to discover they were indeed quite connected to Moses—through their Jewish descent! My father was a great retail merchant in the 1960s and '70s. As such, his employees knew before he did that he was Jewish at heart. His mother, my grandmother, was also a merchant at heart; she helped her family survive the Depression by selling eggs, chickens, and all sorts of farm produce to neighbors. I really wish I knew even more about those times and the stories of my family's lives. Understanding their background and history is important to most human beings. It gives us a sense that we have a deep past.

By contrast, the problem with eliminating God from public life becomes one of objectivity and morality. That does not mean secular people cannot and do not behave morally. Of course they can, and they do. The problem is: how do we choose a moral standard that is common to all men and women, one they are to conform their lives to? What is our reference point? Those very questions troubled even the most brilliant of atheistic philosophers, including Bertrand Russell. Without something bigger than themselves to declare truth, to lay a foundation of right and wrong, Darwin and followers relied on their own intellect and prevailing academic thought to inform their views on race. Without a doubt, they were influenced by what they observed in the world. But the most brilliant people in the world have often been brilliantly wrong.

The problem of slavery is far from limited to the United States. There is a history of slavery in some form for nearly all of recorded history. Simply stated, it was a common practice that was institutionally recognized by most societies. In the fifth to sixth century B.C., between 40 and 80 percent of the population of ancient Greece were slaves. At one point, 25 percent of the population of the Roman empire were slaves.

In the early Islamic states of West Africa, about one-third of the population was enslaved. From around 750 to the 1800s in West Africa, slaves were purchased or captured on the frontiers of the Islamic world and then transported to the major population centers with active slave markets, from which they were widely distributed. From the 11th to 19th centuries, Muslim North African Barbary pirates engaged in raids on European coastal towns to capture Christian slaves to sell at slave markets. It is estimated that across their history, the Barbary pirates captured between 1 million and 1.25 million slaves.

In the mid-1600s, up to three-quarters of Russian peasants, or 13 million to 14 million people, were serfs whose material lives were barely distinguishable from those of slaves. Perhaps another 1.5 million were formally enslaved, with Russian slaves serving Russian masters. Slavery remained a major institution in Russia until 1723, when Peter the Great converted household slaves into house serfs. Russian agricultural slaves were also formally converted into serfs. Russia's 23 million privately held serfs were freed by the Emancipation Reform of 1861. In addition to these notable examples, slavery was practiced in Europe in various forms across all of these time periods.

THERE WAS AN ESTABLISHED PRACTICE AND PATTERN OF SLAVE TRADE AND SLAVERY BETWEEN AFRICA, THE MUSLIM NATIONS OF THE MIDDLE EAST, AND THE CHRISTIAN NATIONS OF EUROPE AND THE AMERICAS. ALL OF THESE REGIONS WERE GUILTY.

To summarize, there was an established practice and pattern of slave trade and slavery between Africa, the Muslim nations of the Middle East, and the Christian nations of Europe and the Americas. All of these regions were guilty. Perhaps surprisingly, slaves were of all races. This was a problem of epic proportion and scale. And it still is. (More on this shortly.)

The beginning of the end of the slave trade in Britain and United States came through an essay written by a brilliant Cambridge student, Thomas Clarkson, in 1785. It was titled: "An essay on the slavery and commerce of the human species, particularly the African, translated from a Latin dissertation." (It is instructive to contrast Clarkson's title with Darwin's.) After completing his award-winning essay, Clarkson claimed that he experienced a spiritual revelation from God that led him to devote the remainder of his life to abolishing slavery. His work would be continued by William Wilberforce, who as a member of Parliament oversaw the passage of Britain's Slave Trade Act of 1807 and finally the Slavery Abolition Act of 1833. Wilberforce died three days after that passage. Both Clarkson and Wilberforce credited a personal spiritual transformation as the reason for their life's work and the power behind it. Both are heros. They represent what one person can do to push back the darkness and literally change the world.

* * * * * * *

In 2017 slavery is, on paper, illegal in every nation on earth. Sadly, tragically, it is still practiced in a variety of ways for a variety of reasons.

A modern-day conversation about race in the United States, in my view, needs to begin with the effect of slavery on racial beliefs and practices. Even though the slave trade ended two hundred years ago and the practice of slavery was abolished in the United States one hundred and fifty years ago, its effects are still with us. What do they look like?

First, slavery violated the most fundamental truth: the established worth and dignity of human beings. When you pervert science and reason to establish and perpetuate a practice that violates truth, there are consequences. Those consequences are far from over in 2017. They may well be getting worse.

Marginalizing an entire people-group diminishes the life, dignity, belief, and self-knowledge of what is possible for each individual and for his or her life. It antagonizes growth, development, and performance. In a totally economic sense, it creates poverty. A poverty that is as much a state of mind as it is a state of income and resources. That state of mind lives both in people who are marginalized and people who practice and perpetuate racism. So the conflicts broaden, offered solutions are contentious, and opinions are all over the place. Generally, most of them miss the mark.

> I WAS BUSTED. I WAS ALSO CURED. HER QUESTION BROUGHT ME TO THE REALITY OF THE DAMAGE OF HATEFUL WORDS. IT IS NOW FIFTY YEARS LATER AND I REMEMBER THAT MOMENT LIKE IT WAS YESTERDAY.

Allow me to tell a very personal story. When I was growing up, every Thursday, Oneta Daniels, an African-American woman, came to our house to help my mom. Oneta was one of the gentlest, kindest, and most loving people I have ever known. During the summer we would often eat lunch together. At every lunch she would have a peanut butter and jelly sandwich. Finally, one day I said, "Oneta, you know that Mom and Dad want you to have whatever you want for lunch that we have in the house." She told me she knew that, but a PBJ was what she liked and wanted. That was just Oneta: a very simple and wonderful woman.

One day—I was about 10—I was in the backyard shooting baskets. My mom came out and, in our conversation, for reasons I will never understand, I used the 'N' word. I could see the disappointment on my mother's face. She didn't scold me or punish me. She did something worse. She looked me in the eyes and said: "How would Oneta Daniels feel if she heard you use that word?" I was busted. I was also cured. Her question brought me to the reality of the damage of hateful words. It is now fifty years later and I remember that moment like it was yesterday.

Oneta deserved more opportunity than she had. However, what she did with the opportunity she was given was love the people in her world. That love made a difference to me, and I bet it made a difference for many others. I hope she felt loved in return.

What I really wish is that she could read these few words and feel my gratitude.

* * * * * * *

Racial prejudice is a problem of the mind and heart. It is profound misunderstanding of the miracle of life and the inherent dignity of each person. Our energy, resources, and efforts need to be directed as if we believe this if we are going to solve these problems. Instead, in extremely misguided efforts, we throw money at the problem and offer programs wrapped in policies that steal life from the very people they are designed to help. If our policy goals are to help marginalized people build self-sufficient, productive, stable lives, then we are failing on almost all levels. We either believe that each person is capable of this kind of life, or we don't.

Unfortunately, the problems of racial tension and animosity don't end here. They continue with the millions of Mexican and other Latino residents who immigrated to the United States illegally. For decades we have had two signs on our southern border with Mexico. The first one says: Keep Out! The second: Help Wanted! The United States has not behaved as a nation that intends to control its borders. This is madness.

This lack of managing our borders heightens the resentment by legal residents for illegal residents. It increases the burden on our health care and educational systems as it keeps the immigrant workers underemployed, without the benefit of law, and outside of the taxable income system. So instead of policies that help race relations, build a more stable culture, and allow a more productive nation, our misguided elected and appointed leaders employ policies that worsen them.

The problem is the same as in so many areas: it is one of mind and heart. It is also one that has a cultural and language barrier. We just don't know each other very well. We don't understand each other well. I could go on to attempt to describe each of the many issues around race in the United States today, but I believe I can summarize them just as well.

African-Americans beginning as slaves. Mexican-Americans beginning as low-income laborers, entangled in border control and immigration problems. Asian-Americans with Eastern beliefs and cultures that are totally integrated as opposed to Western nations where culture, religion, and law are more separate. Muslim Middle Eastern-Americans who are connected to radical Islamic terrorism just because they are Muslim, not because they agree. This is further complicated by Islam as a construct of religion, culture, government, and law, creating yet more barriers for Muslims attempting to peaceably integrate in the West, and more conflict with non-Muslims. We are a pluralistic nation that works very hard to respect that pluralistic nature. However, very few nations attempt to welcome such pluralism into their culture. That often reflects a different kind of racism that exists in those nations.

In India, the lowest caste (class of society) is extremely marginalized and has almost no opportunity to escape the poverty and injustice of that system. So, in this case, classism is essentially no different than racism. In other Asian nations, a person of mixed racial heritage is rejected because they are not of "pure" racial composition, not indigenous to that nation. Plurality becomes a curse in those nations. In Africa, tribal conflicts, wars, and beliefs behave, essentially, as racism as one tribe views the other with great disdain; distorted beliefs fuel the conflicts.

In all of this and in any and every other racial belief we can identify, a pattern emerges. A belief that we begin in our mind takes hold in our heart and becomes ugly and divisive. It never has the foundation or capacity to stand up to penetrating objective investigation. It has no chance to win in the marketplace of ideas, and yet racism still lives on all over the world. What are we to do with that?

Racism begins with the self-deterministic pride of men and women who believe they know best. Whether those ideas begin with the European intellectual elite of Darwin's era who believed in the lie of "favoured races" or Asian honor cultures that believe mixing their pure blood with another ethnic group is "dirty," the error results in diminishing the worth and dignity of a human life. When an American slave owner rationalized the practice of slavery as needed for "economy" and his self-sufficiency, he was violating the very ideals and ideas upon which our Constitution was written and our nation founded. That same Constitution stated that, for perhaps the first time in human history, the sovereignty of each individual was not granted by a king, queen, or government. Rather, it was God Himself who declared our worth.

Until we yield ourselves to the declaration of a holy God who has the position, power, and authority to determine the worth of each and every person He created, we will continue to allow distortion and deception to live in our minds and our hearts, and racism will live on.

ONE TAKEAWAY FROM THIS CHAPTER

All change begins with decisions of the mind, and then with actions that follow, even small ones. Here is something both you and I can do.

Reach out to people of different ethnicities and ask of their experiences of race in their past and present. Doing this over coffee or dinner will make it more social and enjoyable. It is likely they will ask you questions as well. Then you will have a full-tilt dialogue on your hands, and that is a great place to start!

SIX

MONEY

"That which has been is now; and that which is to be hath already been; and God requireth that which is past."

—ECCLESIASTES 3:15 (KJV)

It is difficult to overstate the importance of money. It has so many flavors, so many layers in life. There is what money means to us individually. There is what it means to our family and our family's future. There is what it means to us collectively, to our cities, states, nation, and the world.

We spend a great deal of our life working to have enough of it personally, and because of that hard work, we debate how our collective monies, in the form of tax dollars, should be managed and spent. Money poorly managed can send anyone into a downward spiral of stress and conflict, and eventually destroy what is most precious. In contrast, money well managed can give us the freedom to pursue our life's true calling, take care of our family's needs, and allow us to be generous in uncommon ways.

* * * * * * *

My dad was born in Texas in 1919. He grew up in the Great Depression. His father had a farm near Gatesville, Texas. The local bank repossessed my grandfather's farm during the height of the Depression. He would spend the rest of his life repaying that debt, even when the bank finally told him he didn't have to.

My grandfather was poor in dollars. He was wealthy in responsibility and abundant in character.

What my dad learned from his father was two things: character, and debt travels with danger. He was a master at creating "margin" between his income and the cost of living of our family. He understood money for what it is: a tool. The only debt he had was a mortgage on our house. He paid that off early. His first jobs paid him as little as 25 cents an hour. He had to work multiple jobs to pay the bills. He never forgot what that was like. He had a great work ethic.

What I learned from my dad was the importance of margin, savings, and hard work. I also watched him treat his employees with respect and the understanding that they needed to be paid fairly for their work so they could pay rent and buy groceries and other essentials. Dad remembered the burden of working for very small wages.

That burden was vividly displayed in the story of Hose Smith. Hose was a very old black man who would occasionally do yard work for us. I would do the yard work part of the time, my dad part of the time, and Hose part of the time. Hose could not tell time, read, write, or do much math. Hose charged by the hour. Essentially, he had no way to verify if he was paid properly for his work. I watched my dad pay Hose many times. He always paid him for a little more time than he actually worked just to make sure. My dad knew that Hose needed every dollar to buy groceries and pay the rent . . . just like he needed at one time.

I asked Dad one day if he thought people cheated Hose out of his earned income just because they could. He said that, unfortunately, some people would.

Money is about much more than what it will buy. It is about a mind-set. It is about character, integrity, and the condition of your heart.

* * * * * * *

So, is money good or evil? Is it a wellspring of life or a black hole of insatiable desire, where there is never enough? The truth is, it can be either or both. To gain a more comprehensive perspective, let's go back more than three thousand years in history to look at and listen to one of the wealthiest men of any period in history, King Solomon.

Solomon was the son of King David and the third and final king of a united Israel. It is recorded that in a single year Solomon collected tribute equivalent to 39,960 pounds of gold. His reign lasted for about forty years. He is reported to have had seven hundred wives, three hundred concubines, multiple palaces, flocks of animals, and land too extensive to measure. Solomon possessed anything and everything that money could buy—and then some. He lived to great excess and attempted to lead and manage a household and kingdom that, essentially, was beyond the capacity of any one man.

Solomon's life is described in the Old Testament as one blessed by God; he was a man given great wisdom, wealth, and power. However, as all of those things grew, Solomon looked away from God and his commands and looked to the world to satisfy his desires. He left behind his devotion to the God who had provided, and turned his eyes, heart, and mind to a world that had long since saturated itself in pagan idolatry. The God of the Old Testament had set aside for Himself a people-group, the Jews, who would be separate from the infectious and intoxicating practices of the world, practices counter to God's very nature and will. In making this turn away from God, Solomon set in motion severe consequences for Israel: a divided kingdom and a lessening of power and influence that would eventually give way to the rise of other great nations and their subsequent domination. Solomon's life represented a tipping point for the history of Israel and, in many ways, the rest of the world.

SOLOMON'S LIFE REPRESENTED A TIPPING POINT FOR THE HISTORY OF ISRAEL AND, IN MANY WAYS, THE REST OF THE WORLD.

As Solomon suffered through various consequences of his actions, he was not idle. He recorded his thoughts for us in various places, but especially in Ecclesiastes. The theme he expressed in that small but powerful book of the Bible was futility. In essence, he said: "Vanity of vanities, all is vanity." As someone who had experienced great wealth, power, status, and influence, Solomon concluded that all of those accomplishments did not satisfy the essential needs of his soul. In addition, the accomplishments of work, knowledge, and pleasure were not enough. These things are not without value, but they aren't the chief end of man. The chief end of man is to fear God and keep His commandments. The satisfaction that wealth might bring for a time is fleeting. The mismanagement of it is equally problematic.

In our modern world we tend to focus on current or recent events, ideas, and concepts. We do so at our own peril. The wisdom of men like Solomon often gets left behind. As our culture seeks to revise historical accounts to accommodate postmodern views and standards, we marginalize the importance of world history in our modern lives. As has been said many times: we either learn from history or we repeat it, with all its horrific mistakes. Solomon's was just one life, but it remains an extremely poignant one. We do well to pay attention to it.

As we've stated, we live in a hyperconnected world that continually assaults us with messages. I cannot visit any Internet site without a stream of popup messages relentlessly inviting me to buy something those ads say I must have. In fact, the algorithms at work in cyber-world are so responsive and intelligent that they know what I have viewed on Amazon, trip destinations I have considered, and what purchases I have made. It's not like we really need help in spending money, but we get it anyway, because it works! It has worked so well that, as of 2016, the American consumer, burdened with too much stuff, had rented enough storage space to allow every man, woman, and child living in the United States to stand inside one of those storage units. It is one thing to consume an extravagant amount of material possessions. It is quite another to rent storage to house what we will never use.

Our material desires become the obvious substitution for more meaningful experiences. They are also fun. But in the beginning and in the end, they are merely a state of mind. And they keep us in perpetual conflict. We live way too fast and stressed to enjoy cooking and eating dinner at home, so we are fast food junkies, take-out junkies, and dine-in restaurant junkies. Our often beautifully appointed and equipped kitchens sit idle. And these choices are killing us—literally. It's not news that obesity is an American epidemic. So to counter its effects, we buy diet books, diet products, gym memberships, pay personal trainers to get us into shape, and live in cycles of binge eating followed by extreme dieting. Or we may just choose to remain overweight and suffer the medical consequences, which can be expensive as well. So we use our material wealth to indulge ourselves in ways that make us extremely unhealthy. And then to combat this, we try using more material wealth. All of this happens in an age in which we are relentlessly exposed to images of beautiful people, beautifully fit bodies, and sexual messages that accompany beauty. We use this wealth to buy things that are in conflict with what we really want: life, health, beauty, abundance, and freedom. In truth, we really don't understand or respect money and wealth or the opportunities they can bring.

The concept of money or wealth can be broken down to three perspectives. First, how do we *think* about it? How do we view its purpose and role in our lives? Next, and perhaps even more powerful, how do we *feel* about it? Our emotions run deep and represent the convergence of many life experiences. Those emotions will influence, if not control, how we think about money and wealth. Finally, how we think and *feel* determine how we *act*. So let's journey deeper through the world of wealth and money.

WHAT IF THE BEST LIFE THAT WE COULD CONSTRUCT WAS MEASURED BY FREEDOM AND THE ENJOYMENT OF OUR DAY-TO-DAY LIVES RATHER THAN MATERIAL POSSESSIONS AND THE OBLIGATIONS THAT ACCOMPANY THEM? WOULD WE HAVE LESS STRESS? WOULD WE HAVE MORE TIME FOR ONE ANOTHER?

What if the most influential voices and messages in our lives would take us toward *true* abundance and away from accumulation of material possessions? What if the best life that we could construct was measured by freedom and the enjoyment of our day-to-day lives rather than material possessions and the obligations that accompany them? Would we have less stress? Would we have more time for one another? Would we enjoy life more? Could we be more charitable? Could we build a better future? Of course, the answer to all of these is yes. A different mind-set is what's needed.

Money is a tool. It is one of the many tools we need to build a productive life. It is nothing more or less than that, but we have made it an idol. As an idol, it leads us to counterproductive, destructive, and self-indulgent lives. Let's look at it another way.

If we were thinking, living, and planning from a position of strength, we would look at the time, resources, and opportunities that were available to us and put them to work. If those resources were not available to us, our primary task would be to find a way to gain access to them. This is the story that millions of immigrants to the United States have lived out. It is the story that millions of people from the United States, with almost no means, have brought to life in a free market economy. It has transformed those people who worked wisely and sought the resources they needed. In living this out, we might actually pay it forward and wait on our efforts to produce results. Then we would do that again and again. From the abundance we created, we would then begin to live abundantly. This is a completely different way of thinking! We would put money to work for ourselves rather than making ourselves a servant of money. That takes the power out of the idol! It puts the power back into the purpose of our lives. It puts money to work for us.

Instead, we read *People* magazine rather than the classic books of literature, history, and economics that would help us develop the critical thinking skills and economic perspectives needed in this complex and demanding world. It could even be said that we get our economic training at Walmart, which advertises the slogan "live better for less." So as we make our way out of the store with our groceries that we have just saved on, we pass by racks and racks of cheap pink merchandise that winds up in our carts. The net result is no savings . . . no value . . . no progress . . . no resources left to actually build a life. We don't have to only pick on Walmart; you could substitute Amazon.com, Costco, Sam's, or nearly any retailer of your choice. For those Americans with higher incomes, Wal-Mart might become Nordstroms, or a Toyota Camry might become a Lexus. The result is the same. According to a writer for the Federal Reserve, a 2015 survey found that 47 percent of Americans do not have the funds to cover a $400 emergency event; they would have to borrow money to emerge from the trouble.[1] That is a stunning discovery for a nation described as the wealthiest on earth. How did that happen?

> ACCORDING TO A WRITER FOR THE FEDERAL RESERVE, A 2015 SURVEY FOUND THAT 47 PERCENT OF AMERICANS DO NOT HAVE THE FUNDS TO COVER A $400 EMERGENCY EVENT; THEY WOULD HAVE TO BORROW MONEY TO EMERGE FROM THE TROUBLE.

The United States has been the most economically productive nation in history. It has been a place where, if you are willing to go all in on your dreams, you have a chance. It has been the crossroads of freedom, opportunity, and free markets to allow dreams to prosper. It has demanded hard work and delayed gratification, but it also rewarded those mindsets. Similarly, it punishes the opposite behaviors of self-indulgence and immediate gratification. And the punishment is relentless.

The financial markets are ever curious and in constant search of a place for their capital to perform better. A great example is the industry surrounding consumer credit. The markets clearly recognize the willingness of consumers to use debt to pay for their lives. The financial institutions charge a punishing interest rate to those who make these choices. And amazingly, we do. The return that banks and financial institutions receive on their capital is phenomenal. An individual taking a well-informed look at this would seek ways to be a lender and not a borrower. Instead, most people are buried by this trap. (In fact, the behavior has created an entire industry. Its name—or, his name—is Dave Ramsey, the financial advisor to hundreds of thousands.) We are emotional beings who fail to use logic or proper thinking for the decisions we make.

THE MARKETS CLEARLY RECOGNIZE THE WILLINGNESS OF CONSUMERS TO USE DEBT TO PAY FOR THEIR LIVES. THE FINANCIAL INSTITUTIONS CHARGE A PUNISHING INTEREST RATE TO THOSE WHO MAKE THESE CHOICES.

In a more collective sense, it is, and will be, the nature of free markets to pursue the best yields with the most promising futures. This capital is the jet fuel that helps entrepreneurs create entirely new industries from new ideas that spring to life. The effects were a massive transformation of the United States and world economy in a new and faster-paced dance. To take this transformation worldwide, we built trans-oceanic super highways of fiber-optic cables. Almost overnight, the world went flat as digital files could travel around the world in minutes or even seconds. The digital highways created jobs around the world almost as fast as the files could travel! This was especially true in nations like India, which focused on education and sacrifice. It began one of the greatest creations of wealth the world has ever seen. And that is something to celebrate! No foreign aid program, no political program, no ideological policy could create this new worldwide economic expansion—only the power of free markets.

Transformations rarely occur by themselves. They almost always represent the convergence of multiple forces and trends. These forces include technological developments, infrastructure expansion, labor cost and availability, transportation availability, energy costs, consumer demand in new and established markets, cultural shifts as well as cultural stagnation, changes in the world's financial markets and currencies, oil and gas production technology, and the resulting effects on supply and demand! All of these developments have happened at unprecedented speed.

Free markets are relentless. In this convergence of worldwide developments, the highly responsive markets began to act upon the vast differences in labor costs around a now very flat world. New relationships and new ways of doing business were born. All of a sudden, manufacturing was moved offshore, to Asia, Latin America, and Eastern Europe, and it happened on a historically massive scale. These nations enjoyed the enthusiastic cooperation of multinational corporations, many of which are based here in the United States. If that weren't enough, influence is for sale every day in Washington, D.C. So foreign nations and foreign corporations behaving according to their own interests were and are buyers of influence. This offshoring was destined to happen because of the labor cost differentials, but elected officials are placed in office with a burden to serve the citizens and interests of our nation, not others. So many officials serve their own interests instead. It is tragic.

There has been more and more convergence of these trends, and at an increasingly rapid pace. Offshoring has consequences. As transportation costs and rising labor costs erode profit margins, businesses and individuals begin to respond, once again, to their own interests. They begin to investigate localization of their production. In addition, Americans are increasingly attracted to local sourcing. This includes agricultural products, but also other consumer items. Americans are also motivated to support local and regional jobs with their purchases or to support sustainable environmentally friendly practices. To this mix, we are the beneficiaries of another technological and manufacturing revolution, this one in the form of computer-aided design and computer-aided manufacturing. In real time, producers can design highly complex components, print them in the same room, and assemble them seemingly instantly, in the same building or nearby. For some manufacturing, cheap labor becomes insignificant while the technology, processes, and associated skills drive the process. Of course, this means fewer jobs for real people. It means extremely specific skill sets are needed. It means that actual productivity expands by multiples. Yet all of it also means we have to adapt and change—and quickly—in order to prosper. Americans still have plenty of old ways of thinking that become barriers to change.

In the last fifty years as we have purchased more cars, bigger houses with more appliances, traveled more for work and pleasure, and generally expanded the quality of our lifestyle, the demand for energy, including oil and gas, has grown at significant rates. With this demand we have been importing more and more oil from other nations. This represents a huge outflow of trillions of dollars of capital. We got some of that capital back by selling nations like the Saudis and others our U.S. Treasury notes to finance our increasingly irresponsible federal fiscal debt. Like all debt, that return of our capital comes with a price tag: present-day influence on our policies, future promises of repayment, stress on our currency and financial system. And there is no way to predict how all this will end; there is no precedent. It will require much restraint and decisive and responsible action to create a positive end result.

To add to the complexity of all these converging forces, technology expanded what was possible in oil and gas production through fracking. Within about a decade, the United States began to approach not only self-sufficiency, we became a net exporter. This represented an economic revolution of enormous proportion. The potential long-term effect of keeping trillions of dollars of our capital in our economy and multiplying it by putting it to work through job creation and business creation and expansion is an unspeakable economic advantage. Of course, there are supply and demand imbalances, technological issues, and environmental issues around this mini revolution. They can be solved! Complacency, stagnation, and lethargy are the enemy of solutions. We have the ability to create an entirely new energy future. It is our burden and responsibility to put this historic advantage and new source of economic growth and development to work for our future—not to mention the present. Will we? What are we doing with the wealth we already possess?

* * * * * * *

First, let's define wealth. **Wealth is measured by some store of value.** That store can take the form of currency, commodities, real estate, stocks, bonds, equity in an enterprise, equipment, and many other tangible assets. But it goes a step further: in my view, wealth really has its beginnings in the intangible asset called freedom. A person must be free to think, choose, and act upon their hopes and dreams. They must be free to own private property. They must be free to succeed with all the benefits of success. Also, they must be free to fail with all the consequences of failure. All the tension that pulls and pushes on an individual from these

BUT IT GOES A STEP FURTHER: IN MY VIEW, WEALTH REALLY HAS ITS BEGINNINGS IN THE INTANGIBLE ASSET CALLED FREEDOM. A PERSON MUST BE FREE TO THINK, CHOOSE, AND ACT UPON THEIR HOPES AND DREAMS.

various aspects of freedom is the fuel that overcomes the familiarity and inertia of the status quo. Chasing your dream can be exhilarating. It can also be exhausting—and scary. I have witnessed firsthand what happens to the creativity, dreams, and optimism of people when freedom is stolen from them. Hope disappears. In its place is nothing. No new ideas . . . no new enterprises . . . no new markets . . . no new nothing. That is the enemy of life building, economy building, and nation building. If capital is the fuel of enterprise, then hope is the fuel of human beings.

Wealth is also a function of opportunity. Do we live in an environment of opportunity for great ideas, one that rewards innovation and hard work? Or do we punish it with unnecessary barriers, restrictions, and regulation? The most marginalized of people with the least means to get started are the ones most punished by barriers. Even if the policies that produce these barriers are well intended, they are counterproductive and unjust. In many nations the barriers are cultural and historic. If you don't belong to a certain socioeconomic class, you simply don't get a chance.

Wealth is education. While that is well known, what is enormously frustrating is that we continue to allow other things to dominate our educational system. Today's parents almost single-handedly are handicapping their children to a life of entitled dependency. In addition, today's public education policies are more about ideology than education. We know how to educate children in the most important fundamentals.

Instead of doing that, we convert our schools into social laboratories to experiment with each and every adult-generated ideology we can possibly imagine. This is counterproductive, even tragic. Again, the most disenfranchised children suffer the most—and this puts the future at risk. In fact, if we compare our performance to the rest of the world, we have already fallen. It doesn't seem that way yet to the average American, but it is true.

Fourth and finally, wealth is a mind-set. Most people who have enjoyed success report that almost always the difference between great success, mediocrity, and failure is how a person thinks. That idea is one of the truest things I know. I've experienced in my own life and career the effects of self-limiting thoughts versus thoughts that are energized by possibilities and opportunities. The difference is extraordinary.

Possibility thinking is grounded in abundance, not limitation. It can be learned and mastered. It requires intention. It also requires abandoning many preconceived positions. Abundant thinking requires a willingness to consider some things—many things—that are different from what we currently know. If capital is the fuel of an enterprise, then *how we think is the lever that magnifies efforts and ideas.*

> IF CAPITAL IS THE FUEL OF AN ENTERPRISE, THEN *HOW WE THINK IS THE LEVER THAT MAGNIFIES EFFORTS AND IDEAS.*

The United States is an extraordinarily productive economic machine. From the mid-1980s until the early 2000s, our nation and much of the world went through an unprecedented period of economic growth. It represented the convergence of a technological cycle that was peaking as a demographic cycle of baby boomers was peaking. Yet at the same time, other trends were converging in the opposite direction. The sum total of these trends antagonized the financial well-being of many individuals, institutions, and governments. Again, a brief history is instructive.

According to William Strauss and Neil Howe in *The Fourth Turning*, cycles of history have four parts, or four turnings. The first turning is a high; it brings renaissance to community life. Optimism is at its peak and the mood is "anything is possible." Economic growth is robust and cultural institutions are strong. Post-World War II America is a perfect example of such a high. Next comes an awakening, or the second turning, in which the assumptions and institutions of the high are challenged. This brings new and experimental spiritual and social ideals that attempt to reconcile total fellowship with total autonomy. These are attempts at utopia. The prosperity and security of the high are overtly disdained but—note this—at the same time, covertly taken for granted. The early 1960s to mid-1980s in America represent such an awakening.

The third turning is an unraveling in response to the "liberating" cultural forces set loose in the awakening. Personal satisfaction is high while public trust declines amid a fragmenting culture and harsh debates over values and civic habits. Pleasure-seeking lifestyles coexist with declining tolerance of the same! Guilt increases ... gender differences narrow ... moral debates brew ... and decisive public action becomes diffi-

THE INCOME OF OUR MIDDLE CLASS LAGS AS WE STRUGGLE TO EDUCATE OUR CHILDREN, PAY FOR HEALTH CARE, KEEP UP WITH TECHNOLOGY—THAT WE HAVE A SENSE THAT WE "MUST" OWN, OPERATE, AND PAY FOR, AND IN MULTIPLE DEVICES—AS WELL AS CLOTHING, CARS, AND CASH THAT WE ALSO OBSESS OVER.

cult as community problems are deferred.[2] Does this sound familiar? It should, because we have just lived through—or are living through—such a period. Finally and regretfully, we arrive at the fourth turning: crisis. Our world seems to be positioned on the entrance of this crisis as I write. It may not be, but the polling data says that a large majority of us have a sense that our future is at risk. The income of our middle class lags as we struggle to educate our children, pay for health care, keep up with technology—that we have a sense that we "must" own, operate, and pay for, and in multiple devices—as well as clothing, cars, and cash that we also obsess over. Stagnant incomes, expanding costs of living, and our material desires degrade our financial margin, create debt, and erode our future.

Global terrorism, climate change, relentless and repeating crises of world poverty and, as always, man's inhumanity to man—these things are seemingly without limit. The turning from an unraveling to a crisis reduces national focus to a simple imperative: society must prevail. Unquestionably, we feel a clear and present danger that threatens our well-being. We just don't agree on what it is. What we do agree on is that the financial pressures on most individuals and institutions is threatening their very existence, or at least their existence as we know it.

* * * * * * *

To summarize, the parents of baby boomers were Depression-era children. They saw money as scarce and debt as dangerous. So they were, on the whole, extremely financially responsible and great savers. My generation, the baby boomers, benefited from our parents' frugality with more opportunity. We were more willing to take risks and try new ideas. In general, that created more wealth and brought more opportunities, but it also reduced respect for the value of money as it became easier to come by. As that happened, we spent more, borrowed more, expanded our lifestyle, and saved less. In that process, our children were given more and more material possessions and less and less responsibility to pay for them. It is not unusual for a Millennial to not obtain his or her first job until after completing their college education. And that is a bad idea. Historically in the United States and around the world, children are needed and expected to do some work to contribute to the economic interests of the family. Doing that also happens to prepare them for the responsibilities and challenges of adulthood. That is a really productive idea.

Individually, we have lost our way. Instead of recognizing and using the wealth opportunities available to us, including how we think, we are getting buried by them. By definition, that means we have lost our understanding of the value of money and how to put it to work in our lives. If we can change that, we can create a different future for ourselves and our families.

AT THE SAME TIME THE FEDERAL GOVERNMENT IS BOTH CREATING AND PERPETUATING THE VERY PROBLEMS IT CLAIMS TO BE SOLVING. ONE OF ITS FOUNDATIONAL PROBLEMS IS THAT GOVERNMENT DOES NOT POSSESS AN UNDERSTANDING OR RESPECT FOR THE VALUE OF THE MONEY IT EXTRACTS FROM YOU AND ME IN TAX DOLLARS.

Collectively, our finances are a train wreck of our own creation. The federal government is a grotesque black hole of waste, excess, corruption, paid influence, inefficiency, legislated obstruction, and ideology. At the same time the federal government is both creating and perpetuating the very problems it claims to be solving. One of its foundational problems is that government does not possess an understanding or respect for the value of the money it extracts from you and me in tax dollars. It uses the power of those dollars to expand the wealth and influence of those who hold power inside the Washington, D.C. beltway. The path between "K" street, home of most lobbyists, and our elected officials is worn out.

Your future and my future is for sale every day, all day, by the very people we elect to represent us. Sometimes it is foreign nations that are the buyers. Sometimes it is multinational corporations. Sometimes it is special interest groups. All of the time, it is at our expense. And it clearly represents an immoral and unjust use of the wealth that has been created by so many at such a great price.

Some of us would view the role of the federal government in a more limited way. Those limits would include defense of our nation, providing for a just legal system, creating and operating infrastructure to serve the people, protecting our natural resources, executing foreign policy that serves our nation's interests, and similar fundamental functions that, by and large, average people cannot do alone. By contrast, some of us would envision an expanded role of government that includes many more social programs and governmental interventions in our day-to-day lives.

In either case, if we collectively possessed an abundant understanding and well-informed view of money, wouldn't we demand that it be used in a more prudent way to serve the needs of the people? Some sources report that as much as 70 percent of every dollar allocated for entitlements is consumed in the bureaucracy that manages federal entitlements. Why is that even remotely acceptable? If you sincerely want to help people, why do you promote, support, and allow a system to continue that is so counterproductive to helping the marginalized people it was intended to serve?

So we have a giant beast of federal bureaucracy, paid influence, and corrupt political practices that seems to be immovable. It isn't. The "Brexit vote" by Britons in the summer of 2016 passed by a significant margin. It may be a disaster for Europe and the rest of the world economy; it may not. But people took a stand, made a statement. The phenomenon of the political rise of Donald Trump in 2015-2016 may be something you agree with or something you loathe. Either way, one can't deny the Trump movement was a revolt against status quo and political power as it exists. That status quo includes, but is by no means limited to, unprecedented and unsustainable sovereign debt.

The danger is so real and so apparent that a majority of the British voters were willing to take an enormous economic risk, and a significant number of American voters were willing to nominate an extremely controversial billionaire who was the symbol of an outsider to a corrupt government culture. These unprecedented actions begin and end with economics. They are about freedom and opportunity, about building a life and chasing dreams. They are grounded in the fuel for human beings that we call hope.

And they require that we develop a more informed and abundant view of money and wealth.

Perhaps this journey will take us to the edge of the abyss, where we are forced to answer the ultimate question of wealth. Who truly owns the world's wealth? The answer to that question changes everything. It changed me. It can change you. In it is the very hope that we need to find our way past the abyss to a better present, a better future, and into the loving presence of the One who owns all the wealth of this world and every world, past, present, and future.

ONE TAKEAWAY FROM THIS CHAPTER

Money is a tool and wealth a state of mind. The proper use and application of wealth concepts are necessary for a successful life.

Is money a tool you are using to build a better life or a tool you are using to demolish your life? Is your concept of wealth adequate for an abundant life? Meet with trusted, financially responsible friends and discuss these ideas.

SEVEN

POWER

"Everything can be taken from a man but one thing: the last of the human freedoms—to choose one's attitude in any given set of circumstances, to choose one's own way."[1]
—Victor Frankl, *Man's Search For Meaning*

A conversation about power is really a conversation about influence. Influence is leverage. It is the lever that we apply to the efforts and purposes of our lives. A proper look at power requires that we first define it. Our next question is to determine if we have access to the power we need for our lives. Finally, we must ask the question of what will we do with the power we possess. This in-depth look at the concept of power may seem simple. It is anything but. The inherent complexity of human beings keeps the struggle for power a dynamic and interesting story. The story ranges from tragedy to triumph.

Every person, regardless of how meager their circumstances, possesses some degree of power over their life. Often, they simply don't act on it. In a world in which so many people feel hopeless, helpless, and stuck, power—personally and collectively—is often a missing ingredient. It is the fuel for the engine of change, growth, and opportunity. So often, we just don't recognize the power available to us. We tend to have a distorted view of what power really is and how we are to use it.

Power is defined in multiple ways. The first definition I came across in Wordbook, my phone dictionary app, was: "The possession of controlling influence." Similarly, wordbook offers this definition: "Possession of the qualities required to do something or get something done." No individual, organization, institution, or nation can be without power for long and prosper. Most of us would agree that our nation and our world have been mired in conflicting and competing worldviews for far too long. Those views include political theory, sexuality, race and origin, religious belief and expression, economics, and many, many other disputes. It is going to take a great revolution of thinking and living to change things.

But every great movement begins with the power of one. That means *me*. That means *you*. Let's start with what it means individually to each of us.

* * * * * * *

Victor Frankl was a Viennese psychiatrist imprisoned in the Holocaust at Auschwitz. He wrote a book after his liberation from that brutal and inhumane concentration camp. *Man's Search For Meaning* is one of the most famous books of the twentieth century. In my view, every human being taking a breath should be required to read this book. In it, Frankl described the misery of life as a prisoner during the Holocaust and how much human necessity and dignity was taken from the lives of the innocent human beings held captive at camps like these. In spite of every inhumane act forced on the prisoners, in spite of every shred of human decency that was removed, in spite of starvation, beatings, and a culture of death, what survived in Victor Frankl was . . . the power to decide

HE CHOSE TO ACCESS THE POWER AVAILABLE TO HIM THROUGH WORSHIP AND BEING CONNECTED TO HIS CREATOR AS WELL AS THE DISCIPLINE OF NOT YIELDING TO THE DAY-TO-DAY SUFFERING HE ENDURED. HE WAS COMMITTED TO THE LIFE HE WAS GOING TO LIVE AFTER AUSCHWITZ.

what he would think in the privacy of his own mind. It was there that he created a future worth living for. Intentionally, privately, quietly . . . and completely unknown to his captors, Frankl maintained the power of his own mind. He chose to access the power available to him through worship and being connected to his Creator as well as the discipline of not yielding to the day-to-day suffering he endured. He was committed to the life he was going to live after Auschwitz—this was a life he built every day, all day long, in his mind. The power he needed existed internally in his heart, soul, and mind. It began with a decision: a decision to *live*. Frankl made this decision every day. If you and I are going to truly live, life will require the same of us.

The power I am attempting to describe is the result of decisions or commitments you and I make in the places where we feel the deepest, dream the biggest, and hope so strongly that it aches. Decisions are the substance of leadership. Leadership always begins with first influencing and leading *oneself*. My favorite definition of leadership is: Leadership is about taking a position and maintaining that position in the midst of pressure to do otherwise. Think of the pressure on Frankl and his fellow prisoners. It was enormous, relentless. But if you have already decided to *live*, regardless of today's events . . . to succeed, regardless of today's barriers . . . to empty yourself to the world around you regardless of your wavering resolve . . . then you have determined your destination by simply deciding that your only option is to live. If you are really bold then you might even risk living the biggest, brightest, boldest life you can envision.

That life begins today, but it takes doing the things required of that kind of life. In Auschwitz the average person died. In our world today, the average person regresses to a life of regret, a life defined by *what if*. A life of missed opportunity. I am asking you to throw away usual and customary. I am asking you to not give in to the relentless pressures of the world to lower your standards, but to design and build a mind-set that supports something bolder. Frankl, essentially void of visible power, lived a powerful internal life and reaped external consequences. He talked prisoners out of suicide, pleading with them to die at the hands of their captors so that there would one day be meaning from their death when all the atrocities were discovered. He survived the Holocaust to create an entirely new school of thought in the field of psychiatry. *Man's Search For Meaning*, published about sixty years ago, endures strongly to this day, and has been read by millions. All of this power came from the provision of Frankl's Creator, who granted him a strong purpose and the discipline to take every thought captive in spite of his suffering. And perhaps it was the suffering itself

> I AM ASKING YOU TO THROW AWAY USUAL AND CUSTOMARY. I AM ASKING YOU TO NOT GIVE IN TO THE RELENTLESS PRESSURES OF THE WORLD TO LOWER YOUR STANDARDS, BUT TO DESIGN AND BUILD A MIND-SET THAT SUPPORTS SOMETHING BOLDER.

that produced the power to live an extraordinary life.

What Frankl and so many others like him have taught us is that what we need is *inside* of us. It lives in the depths of our being. In the places that we feel the deepest, dream the biggest, hurt the most, and hope so much that it aches. It is hard to get us to go to that place unless we are forced to. Brokenness has its advantages and uses, even if reaching that state is exquisitely painful.

* * * * * * *

Dietrich Bonhoeffer, born in 1906, was a German Lutheran pastor. Bonhoeffer was well known for his staunch opposition to the Nazi regime, his vocal opposition to the genocidal persecution of the Jews, and his criticism of the state-controlled church that arose from Nazi manipulation. His most well-known book, *The Cost of Discipleship*, was written at a time he was teaching and operating underground seminaries in small towns and villages around Germany. The book was a study of Christ's Sermon on the Mount. During his training and experiences at Union Theological Seminary in New York, Bonhoeffer began to see things "from below"—from the perspective of those who suffer oppression. As a professor of theology, Bonhoeffer was positioned to comment and act on the suffering of the victims of oppression in World War II Germany as well as racial oppression in the United States. He saw that he possessed a certain amount of power he could utilize even in the face of the overwhelming totalitarian regime of Nazi Germany. He was an educator, activist, and voice of opposition to the church establishment that had capitulated to the evil Nazi ideology. It cost Bonhoeffer his life. He was executed by hanging on April 9, 1945 at Flossenburg concentration camp—two weeks before its liberation by soldiers of the United States Army.[2]

Seventy-two years later I am writing about and learning

from his life. Martin Luther King Jr. and the civil rights movement, the anti-apartheid movement in South Africa, and the Eastern European anti-communist democratic movement in the Cold War—these all credited Bonhoeffer with being influential and inspirational in their struggle for freedom and justice. True power is not limited to the here and now; it is transcendent. It can change lives, and our world, long after its day. Bonhoeffer's use of the power available to him lives on in stark contrast to many of the current views of power. He was driven by deeply held convictions that grew from his faith in a God who is just, loving, and merciful.

We have all seen so much abuse of power. Many had childhoods in which a parent abused his or her parental authority. The idea of power may sound or feel frightening. Others have suffered under superiors at work, men or women who misused their power. The result is usually resentment. There are so many ways power is abused. These kind of experiences easily create a view that power is just something that someone uses for his or her own selfish and destructive desires.

The world views power in terms of position, force, control, and authority. It says that the loudest voice, the strongest voice, and the most influential voice wins in an argument. A postmodern world believes that words and language have no inherent meaning; rather, they are simply instruments of power by those in power. Further, a postmodern world believes that there is no such thing as reality. Truth and reality are simply illusions. There is no common or shared reality that, collectively, we can conform our minds and lives to. When this is the prevailing thought, each individual has license to invent his or her own version of reality. That is the power of a postmodern world, but at the same time one of the reasons so many people are bewildered by what they see and experience around them. We struggle to reconcile a created reality with what we know to be true from our education, historical accounts, upbringing, and life experiences. If you attempt to take a position that is antagonistic to almost any newly created postmodern "reality," you get worked. And this can be ugly.

Let me offer an example. The world is besieged with terrorism. The severity, frequency, and geography of these murderous acts appear to be increasing at an alarming rate. They have changed our world and disrupted our lives, institutions, and peace of mind. They are designed to do those very things. All terror events are barbaric, inhuman, immoral. The killing is senseless and its victims random. Terrorists are willing to put noncombatant children and adults at risk to carry out their missions. The organizations of terror exist on every continent and in most every nation. They go by different names, such as ISIS, Al Qaeda, Boko Haram, Hezbollah, and Hamas, but there are really too many to list. And if the free world completely defeated them tomorrow, new organizations and affiliations would be created almost instantly. The idea that terror is a static entity is foolish, reckless, and in conflict with what an objective investigation reveals. Terrorism is not even the people who carry it out. It is about the ideology that gives it life.[3]

A defining moment in the history of terrorism was September 11, 2001. Life as we knew it changed on that date. That day began many public conversations about terrorism, what it means, and how to do battle with it. Those conversations came from both the terrorists themselves and the leaders of the free world. The terrorists were clear: they were practicing jihad as their duty in worshiping and serving Allah, their God, with the ultimate goal of spreading Islam and the Islamic way of life to the rest of the world. Regardless of the group, its affiliations, or its country of origin, what drives this mind-set is the same: expansion of Islamic ideology and Islamic domination of the nations of the world. It's clear that radical jihad is a clear and present danger to the world now and in the future. There is something in Islam that gives jihadists the authority and instruction to carry out acts of terror.

How has the postmodern world responded? First, there was a military response. In hindsight, that looks like an enormous mistake. No nation has ever tamed Iraq, Afghanistan, or neighboring countries. In fact, the internal conflict between the Sunni and Shiites in Iraq renders the nation incapable of stable governance. The Taliban in Afghanistan produces a similar instability. Interestingly, the Sunnis and Shiites have been in conflict since Mohammed's death in 632.[4] The history of both groups is armed conflict with one another that began with the disagreement of who would lead Islam after Mohammed's death. Given all of that, what were the messages from our leaders, including then President George W. Bush and other conservatives?

> THOSE CONVERSATIONS CAME FROM BOTH THE TERRORISTS THEMSELVES AND THE LEADERS OF THE FREE WORLD. THE TERRORISTS WERE CLEAR: THEY WERE PRACTICING JIHAD AS THEIR DUTY IN WORSHIPING AND SERVING ALLAH, THEIR GOD, WITH THE ULTIMATE GOAL OF SPREADING ISLAM AND THE ISLAMIC WAY OF LIFE TO THE REST OF THE WORLD.

- Islam is a religion of peace.
- Radical Islamic terrorism does not represent true Islam; it is a perversion.
- The Muslims that support jihad are a small minority.
- In combatting terrorism, profiling terrorists is judgmental, immoral, and unacceptable.

In writing this, I have been flooded with the sense that I

need to address how a faithful Muslim must feel as he or she attempts to live out their faith in an age of terrorism and overt jihad. As I wrote this chapter in 2016, ISIS claimed responsibility for a Bagdad bombing that killed two hundred people, many of whom were children. We could expect that all of the killed were Muslim; there are essentially no Christians left in Iraq. A devoted mainstream Muslim must be overwhelmed with a multitude of painful emotions, frustration, anger, and bewilderment. I know that most of them do not find justification for these acts in their faith. They must feel extremely marginalized. We need mainstream Muslims to display the courage to fight terrorism inside their community of faith. They will likely suffer consequences for doing this. Similarly, we need non-Muslims to recognize, accept, and build relationships with their Muslim neighbors who stand against this kind of violence. We need to help them peacefully coexist in our Western nations. Assimilation is difficult; they must feel they live completely outside of our culture and its institutions.

It must be recognized that radical Islamic terrorists work extremely hard to blend in to the culture and community around them, so it is quite difficult to identify and separate those with radicalized views from those who do not have the same beliefs.

I am proposing that we live out the idea that each human being is made in the image of God according to His likeness. As such, we are to value one another with the greatest worth and dignity that we are capable of, regardless of our belief system, nation of origin, or culture. That does not mean that we should surrender everything that we hold precious, the inalienable rights granted by our Creator, in order to peacefully coexist. It means that we should actually live according to that belief and expect all our neighbors to do the same. It won't be easy or feel natural, but it will be critical for progress.

I invite you to actually study Islam. First, listen to mainstream Sunni clerics describe their precepts and foundational beliefs. Next, look around the world at Muslim majority nations and see how they live out the construct called Islam. Then read the history of Mohammed and the spread of Islam. (There are many credible sources written by highly credentialed and respected academics.) Finally, listen to the terrorists themselves. And consider this question: who are we to argue with the reasons they give for what they do? Many of them are sacrificing their own lives for the sake of carrying out their mission. Do you really believe that they would volunteer to die unless they believed they were acting on behalf of Allah in the exact way that he commanded? In other words, there is something in Islam that allows the most pure devotees of the ideology to perpetrate terror on every continent and view it as their obligation.

The messages of those both for and against Islam are verbalized often and with great authority, from people of position, power, and influence. In addition, they are repeated and expanded by individuals with significant media platforms. Unfortunately, many of these preferred realities are not based in fact, as evidenced in accurate historical accounts, nor are they representative of the modern-day practices of Muslim majority nations. But . . . they have worked. The vast majority of Western people believe many of these messages, generally without ever investigating the facts. These are perfect examples of postmodern influences on today's people. Remember, words and language are viewed as instruments of power, not as vehicles of communication to bring meaning to human relationships.

Perpetuating these constructed beliefs prevents us from understanding our enemy, their motivations and behavior, and understanding their end game. These beliefs are reckless. They contribute to the continuation of radical Islamic terrorism. They have become so distorted that in 2016 our military and security agencies were not allowed to use certain words that describe terrorism. These include *jihad, radical Islamic terrorism*, and other words that connect terrorism with Islam. I do not recall ever studying the successful outcome of a war in which the victor did not develop an excellent understanding of the enemy. Generally, when we attempt to understand all of this madness, we view it through the lens of political correctness. But it goes much deeper—these postmodern ideas are powerful and run quite deeply in us.

> GENERALLY, WHEN WE ATTEMPT TO UNDERSTAND ALL OF THIS MADNESS, WE VIEW IT THROUGH THE LENS OF POLITICAL CORRECTNESS. BUT IT GOES MUCH DEEPER— THESE POSTMODERN IDEAS ARE POWERFUL AND RUN QUITE DEEPLY IN US.

My critique is with the Western postmodern approach to the construct of Islam. It is not with the people of Islam. Many Muslims are in complete disagreement with terrorism and want to end it. Many Muslim people sincerely want to integrate into the Western nations where they reside or live and to do so with greater freedom than in their nation of origin. And to be fair, there are many Muslims who seek the same endgame of Islamic expansion, but believe in nonviolent strategies and tactics. In either case, it is the nature of the Islamic construct to define and control all aspects of life while at the same time actively working to make each nation a Muslim majority.

There are other stories of power related to this central idea of Islam. In essentially all cases, a Muslim leaving Islam will be rejected by and isolated from his or her family. In most Muslim majority nations, it is a punishable crime for a Muslim to leave his or her faith.In a few countries, it is a capital offense. [5] In these nations, Islam is a totalitarian ideology with little to no room for dissenting views or beliefs. The state,

IN MOST MUSLIM MAJORITY NATIONS, IT IS A PUNISHABLE CRIME FOR A MUSLIM TO LEAVE HIS OR HER FAITH. IN A FEW COUNTRIES, IT IS A CAPITAL OFFENSE.

holding all the power, keeps its foot on the neck of its citizens. The lack of freedom to think, choose, and believe as one sees fit is disturbing. It is yet another display of power meant to maintain total control over the people.

Then there is the power possessed by terrorists themselves. I have not lost a loved one in a terrorist event. I can't imagine the pain and anger I would feel. In a much smaller sense, every time I go through security in an airport, I am reminded that it exists solely because radical Islamic terrorists have killed thousands of people with commercial aircraft. To my knowledge, no other group has done this. We spend hundreds of billions of dollars annually in an effort to secure our aircraft and airports. But a 2016 bombing in Turkey reminded us that we have not actually done that. In fact, we give the TSA an impossible task of screening millions of travelers each year. They do their best, but fall short. In this story of power, terrorists use their muscle to instill fear, disrupt the function of institutions and private enterprise, and distract free people from important tasks in their lives.

I have used a very volatile and controversial example to make my point. However, radical Islam seems to be the greatest source of conflict and instability around our world. As such, it is so important to get this right, and we are getting it so wrong. The further we travel down this road of constructing a reality around Islam that is not true, the more error we introduce, and the further we move from an accurate understanding, effective strategies, and solutions. In this ever-worsening error, we continue to pay an enormous price.

* * * * * * *

The most powerful conversation I ever had was with Dr. Michael Stuart. We had been casual friends for many years. Mike had been a dedicated and trusted leader in my profession locally, statewide, and nationally. The list of people who loved Mike Stuart is too long to include in this book or any book. Quite simply, he was a category of one.

Mike was diagnosed with melanoma. In typical Mike style, he waged an enormous battle with that very destructive and invasive disease. In the winter of 2015, after many remissions and relentless treatments, lesions were discovered in his brain. Mike would return to Baylor hospital in Dallas for treatments. I saw him on the first Friday in February at the annual meeting of the Southwest Academy of Restorative Dentistry following one of his treatments. I sought him out intentionally. I will always be thankful for this experience. It was a gift from God. We talked for maybe fifteen minutes. In that conversation I learned Mike was ready for whatever was in front of him. I heard and felt love, gratitude, extreme faith in the God who had given him life in the first place and, most amazingly, peace. It was the kind of peace that defies all understanding. Instead of me comforting Mike, he comforted me with his words and, more importantly, his being.

Mike died two weeks later. There were more than eight hundred people at his funeral. It was the longest funeral I have ever attended because so many people had so much to say and just could not stop talking about him. Mike lived a powerful life. It is the type of power any of us can exercise. It is the power of one.

* * * * * * *

Let's leave the ideas of this world and turn to ideas from another. In this different world, justice, hope, and restoration are its framework, foundations, and methodology. On these things a person can build or rebuild a life, family, culture, or nation. They are packed with wisdom, insight, and vision.

The Old Testament prophet Isaiah recorded a clear picture of how we are to exercise the power we possess, be it great or small. Isaiah lived about 700 B.C. He is and was perhaps the most popular of the Jewish prophets. Chapter 42 is widely held to be speaking about the coming Messiah:

Here is my servant, whom I uphold, my chosen one in whom I delight; I will put my spirit on him and he will bring justice to the nations. He will not shout or cry out, or raise his voice in the streets. A bruised reed he will not break, and a smoldering wick he will not snuff out. In faithfulness he will bring forth justice; he will not falter or be discouraged till he establishes justice on earth. In his teaching the islands will put their hope (vv. 1-4, NIV).[6]

In this beautiful passage Isaiah describes a servant chosen by God in whom God finds delight. Think about that for a moment: the being of the servant is so good that it brings delight to the Father, and that being will represent how the servant will serve—with all the approval, power, and authority of the God of Heaven, and in a way that will bring forth justice and hope for all people to the ends of the earth. We don't often associate justice with hope, but in a world where there is so much injustice, just outcomes bring hope to the oppressed. The passage goes on to describe how this servant will live out the power and authority he has been given—gently, humbly, quietly—and all while possessing all the might of Heaven. In the time of Isaiah and in much of history since, a king or queen would arrive with great fanfare and a legion of soldiers showing force and position. But *this* leader/servant would be different. His use of the power he was given would be extremely countercultural.

"A bruised reed he will not break . . ." Reeds, in the time of Isaiah, were useful for many things. You could weave them together and make a roof, boat, or container of some kind. You could sharpen the end of the reed, dip it in ink, and write. But if the reed was broken by external force, it became less useful, if not useless. *"A smoldering wick he will not snuff out . . ."* Lamps in Isaiah's day had water under the oil and wick as a protective measure to put out the flame when the oil was used up. The flame of the lamp would die when it had exhausted all the internal energy it had in the oil. So what we obviously gather from this passage is that this servant will not use his power to further dominate the person who is broken by external forces or exhausted from within—rather he will use his power and authority to *restore* them . . . to make them whole again . . . full of life and energy. And in his pursuit of restoring you and I, he will not stop or be discouraged regardless of the barriers and resistance the world brings or that you and I bring.

Isaiah revealed a view of power and its use in the context of a servant who restores. He says, in the quietness and privacy of your own internal being, God will use the unlimited power and authority that He has to restore your brokenness and renew your energy. In essence, God stands in the gap for you and me. Restoration of those who are broken from external burdens and internal exhaustion is the work of great leaders. It is their greatest gift. It is also mostly absent in contemporary public life. Power, according to Isaiah, is not at all what we think or see in our world.

I write this chapter in a city

> RESTORATION OF THOSE WHO ARE BROKEN FROM EXTERNAL BURDENS AND INTERNAL EXHAUSTION IS THE WORK OF GREAT LEADERS. IT IS THEIR GREATEST GIFT.

besieged by those in pursuit of power, Washington, D.C. It is such a magnificent city with an extraordinary history. It also attracts countless numbers of people seeking more power, influence, status, fame and, of course, wealth. But I wonder if they really want to lead. I wonder if they really want to serve. I wonder if they really want to use their lives to restore people who are broken, exhausted, and just trying to find their way. If they want to provide true justice. When justice is gone, so is hope.

Joe Batten, author of *Tough-Minded Leadership*, wrote: "The first and last task of a leader is to keep hope alive. The hope that we can find our way to a better world despite our own self-indulgence, inertness, and wavering resolve." Batten is saying that, ultimately, providing hope should be the end product of a leader and his or her use of power.[7]

Frankl used the only power that he possessed, his private thought life, gaining his strength from the God he worshiped, to craft a meaningful plan to live and help others either die with meaning or live for meaning that was to come when the truth of the Holocaust was exposed. After his liberation, he founded a new school of psychiatry based on what he learned in the hell of the Holocaust—just as he planned every single day during his captivity. Bonhoeffer used the power of his unyielding faith in a God of justice, love, and mercy to push back the darkness of Nazi Germany. It cost him his life. But the powerful way Bonhoeffer lived has inspired millions and forced the church and world to examine their failure to intervene in the evil they were witnessing.

In great contrast, postmodern thought demands that we accept the meaningless of life as reality. Therefore, power is simply an instrument one uses to expand his or her interests. In a postmodern world, words and language do not possess inherent meaning; they are instruments of power and influence. Islam views power as submission, which is the actual meaning of the word *Islam*. In this construct, submission is total in all aspects of life. Power in this sense is all-consuming.

Isaiah, as pointed out, speaks of a completely different view of power. He spins a story of restoration and renewal of those who are broken and exhausted. In this story, we find justice. From justice, we experience hope.

ONE TAKEAWAY FROM THIS CHAPTER

How will you exercise the power available to you? You have the power of one. It includes the power to take every thought captive regardless of your circumstances, just like Victor Frankl, just like Michael Stuart. You have the power to love, even when someone is extremely difficult to love. Nothing is more powerful than that. Love includes belief, acceptance, forgiveness, compassion, and sometimes toughness. All of these things have the capacity to provide hope, the fuel of life.

The light of hope in a human heart has the power to push back the darkness one person at a time. Journal your thoughts on how you can use your power of one to change the world around you.

EIGHT

SEXUALITY

*"Joy is not a substitute for sex; sex is very
often a substitute for joy. I sometimes wonder
whether all pleasures are not substitutes for joy."*[1]

—C.S. LEWIS, *SURPRISED BY JOY*

We live in a sexually obsessed culture. Even a superficial
look at images, strategies, and messages in the media will con-
vince you of the hypersexualized nature and focus of our lives.
It leaves none unscathed; it spans all ages and socioeconomic
groups.

What began as a sexual revolution by the baby boomers
was continued by Generation X and is coming to full actual-
ization in today's Generation Y. It is not that sexuality is a new
frontier; in fact, it is as old as humanity. It is that its importance in contemporary culture and to the individual lives in
that culture has moved off the charts. I don't know that there
is an era to compare it with. I am well aware of ancient pagan
ritual practices, temple prostitution, and the culture of Rome
during the height of its power. But today, we have the benefit
of science, medicine, history, and anthropology to teach us

better. It seems we have learned nothing from all of the history available to us.

It seems that I learned very little from the failures in my life until the pain was great enough to force the lessons on me. As with almost all change, we have been slowly marinating in a potion that is relentless and all-consuming, an environment of expanding sexual norms. As such, it may not seem like a drastic change. It is. Is this what we want? It seems so. Will it lead us to human thriving and abundant life? I don't think so. It has not led me to those outcomes, and I have tried.

I WRITE AS SOMEONE WHO HAS LIVED THROUGH IT ALL—AND EXPERIENCED MUCH OF IT. I HAVE HAD SEVERAL FRIENDS DIE FROM AIDS. I HAVE TOO MANY FRIENDS WHO HAVE HAD ABORTIONS OR UNPLANNED TEENAGE PREGNANCIES AND ARE SUFFERING THE EMOTIONAL CONSEQUENCES.

I want to ask you to consider the role of sexuality in your life and our culture. I also want to take a look at how we got here. Things aren't exactly *Leave It to Beaver* anymore.

I grew up in the middle of the sexual revolution of the 1960s. I was a full participant. As such, I am not thinking and writing from outside these developments. I write as someone who has lived through it all—and experienced much of it. I have had several friends die from AIDS. I have too many friends who have had abortions or unplanned teenage pregnancies and are suffering the emotional consequences. Sadly, I have personally experienced failed marriages. All of those experiences are connected to ways of living and behaving that resulted from a revolution of total sexual freedom.

Any chapter I write on sexuality has to include something of my own experience. In his marvelous book *Surprised by Joy*, C.S. Lewis described himself as being "as nearly nonmoral on that subject (sexuality) as a human creature can be." I wouldn't go quite that far in describing myself at different points in my life, but the description comes close enough. In contrast, God has revealed His plan for human sexuality to all of us. That plan, and His hand in my life, protected me. Not because of my obedience, but because of His providence. He removed so many opportunities. He altered the course of so many events. At times, He eliminated the energy required. There was so much that could have been so destructive and so devastating. Situations that I would have said yes to, given the opportunity, simply never materialized. It is not possible to measure the benefit to me and the difference made in my life. God simply provided boundaries, limits, and direction that limited the damage in my life.

In essence, God was protecting me from *me*. He was providing an unchanging point of light for me in a world that never stops changing, never stops spiraling in a chaotic swirl of social entropy. He never abandoned me in spite of myself. Perhaps that is why they call His grace amazing.

* * * * * * *

Human beings, for a great part of our history, have been drawn to or attempted to create a utopia. It seems that there is something inherent in being human that makes the thought of utopia attractive. Merriam-Webster Dictionary provides this background: "In 1516, English humanist Sir Thomas More published a book titled *Utopia*.[2] It compared social and economic conditions in Europe with those of an ideal society on an imaginary island located off the coast of the Americas. More wanted to imply that the perfect conditions on his fictional island could never really exist, so he called the place

Utopia, a name he created by combining the Greek words *ou* (meaning 'no') and *topos* (meaning 'place'). The earliest generic use of *utopia* was for an imaginary and indefinitely remote place. The current use of *utopia*, referring to an ideal place or society, was inspired by More's description of Utopia's perfection."[3] Merriam-Webster Dictionary defines utopia as "an imaginary place in which the government, laws, and social conditions are perfect."[4] But the sad truth is, almost all efforts toward creating a utopia result in a dystopia. The carnage in these dystopias can be devastating.

The sexual revolution that began in the early 1960s was really part of a grander utopian effort to reorder our cultural norms and institutions. It did not occur in isolation, but rather was a central piece of the convergence of many developments and trends. Remember that Strauss and Howe, in *The Fourth Turning*, identified repeating cycles of history that they divided into four stages, or turnings. (The concept was developed in chapter six of this book, Money, but let's apply it to the sexual revolution here.) The first turning began with young adults returning from World War II who were children of the Depression, which was the crisis of the previous cycle. They were the heroes of a great war, returning triumphant. They established great institutions, robust economic growth, and significant power and influence in the world. Their children grew up in the 1950s and '60s with economic stability and a bright future. These children saw the world in a different way than their parents, however, and began a second turning, an awakening, a challenge to the

> THE SAD TRUTH IS, ALMOST ALL EFFORTS TOWARD CREATING A UTOPIA RESULT IN A DYSTOPIA. THE CARNAGE IN THESE DYSTOPIAS CAN BE DEVASTATING.

assumptions and institutions of the day; this turning began around 1960. It brought new and experimental spiritual and social ideals that attempted to reconcile total fellowship with total autonomy. Again, these are essentially attempts at utopia. It's important to know that the prosperity and security of the high are overtly disdained but covertly taken for granted. Many of these challenges began with modern and postmodern philosophers who said that God was dead, meaning was lost, and the chief end of man was pleasure. In other words, sex, drugs, and rock and roll ruled. Proponents of this revolution explored mind-expanding drugs and sexual experiences without restraint. A visit to the intersection of Haight and Ashbury streets in San Francisco on any given day in the 1960s would have produced a firsthand look at that life. LSD and other hallucinogenic, mind-expanding drugs ruled, but their long-term effects would be tragic.

To complete this sexual revolution, medicine would be needed to expand and improve birth control methods; it was developed. The legal system would need to create unrestricted access to pregnancy termination. In 1973, the Supreme Court's Roe vs. Wade ruling did just that. Medicine also needed to provide simple and cost-effective therapies for sexually transmitted diseases. Again, it did. Antibiotics were effective against the diseases of the day. They no longer are.

Parallel to all this, women took the feminist movement to new heights as they sought an expansion of the role of women in the business world, more freedom—especially sexual freedom—and just and equitable treatment in all aspects of life. Although there is still debate today about income equality and opportunity for women, clearly the feminist revolution brought about extraordinary change. It continues to this day. While there are aspects of this movement to celebrate, it also has added to the pressure, busyness, and complexity of life for most working women. Their children are involved in more activities than ever. Their careers and their husbands' careers often include travel. Thus, many women find themselves exhausted from the pace of change as they attempt to build careers and be great wives and mothers.

In addition, and perhaps more significantly in this utopian effort, was the issue of race and racism. Slavery, and the racism connected with it, is one of the ugliest facets of the history of the United States. At its core, it is abandonment of the most fundamental principle declared by our Creator, that each of us is made in His image, according to His likeness, with all of the dignity and worth that only He can bestow. (For a more detailed look at this issue, see chapter five of this book.)

When you violate truth and dehumanize human beings, you begin a downward spiral of beliefs, attitudes, and culture. Both economic poverty and poverty of mind result.

Under Strauss and Howe's model, the third turning comes next. This is an unraveling in response to the "liberating" cultural forces set loose in the awakening and the utopian efforts of the second turning. Personal satisfaction is high while public trust declines amid a fragmenting culture and harsh debates over values and civic habits. We can say this is precisely what took place in the 1980s and '90s.

ESSENTIALLY, THE TECHNOLOGICAL REVOLUTION HAS BROUGHT ALMOST ANY TYPE OF VISUAL SEXUAL EXPERIENCE TO ALMOST ANY AND EVERY DEVICE; JUST TWENTY-FIVE YEARS AGO THIS WAS NOT POSSIBLE. ALL OF THIS HELPED FUEL THE PURSUIT OF SEXUAL EXPERIMENTATION, EXPANSION, AND EVENTUALLY THE DESTRUCTION OF ALL SEXUAL NORMS.

Although we struggled to identify the specifics, we had a sense that much of our culture was moving in the wrong direction and our future looked worse than our past.

In this third turning, we truly became a sexually obsessed culture. In business, sex sells, and it is used to sell us everything. Selling sex on the Internet became an enormous industry, and to this day it occupies more bandwidth than any other activity. It is, by every definition, an epidemic that violates most moral and ethical constructs as well as many laws. Essentially, the technological revolution has brought almost any type of visual sexual experience to almost any and every device; just twenty-five years ago this was not possible. All of this helped fuel the pursuit of sexual experimentation, expansion, and eventually the destruction of all sexual norms. As every form of media was liberated from restraint, we went all in to identify with and embrace new ways of living that were powerfully attractive. We also began to increasingly identify ourselves with our own sexuality, and our lives reflected a pattern of increased sexual experiences in increasingly experimental ways. We were watching them in every form of media; how could we resist in our own lives? Even practices previously not imaginable became commonplace; virtual sex has become a way of life for far too many.

Strauss and Howe's model finally arrives at a fourth turning: crisis. It could have been the financial crisis of 2008-2009. The economic utopia was suddenly becoming a dystopia, with nations and individuals drowning in debt. The European Union and the Euro were poised to intensify the storm of the United States investment bank failures, and a number of nations around the globe failed financially. Nobody knows how all of this will play out, but it surely won't be pretty.

The financial aspect was just the tip of the iceberg. We face a crisis of culture. The institution of family has long suffered the damage of divorce rates higher than 50 percent. More babies are born out of marriage now than at any point in history.

All of this produces demographics in which more than 70 percent of children are growing up in single parent households that are all too often poor. There are always inspiring stories of families and children who overcome the difficulties of single parent homes. But mostly, those in such environments experience more struggles and have a much harder time building productive lives. Essentially, the question becomes: Are our children and grandchildren, individually and collectively, becoming the kind of productive citizens a great nation requires?

****

In 2016, we seem to be approaching the limits of self-determinism. We also seem to be approaching the limits to our solutions and revolutions. What seems to be underlying all of our substantial efforts to overturn the institutions that previously determined much of our identity is a relentless desire to determine our own reality, especially our sexuality. All of these efforts at utopianism traveled together. So it is helpful to look at some of these. But sexuality defines them all.

As we attacked racism in the 1960s, Dr. Martin Luther King Jr. gave us the answer in his "I Have a Dream" speech. He dreamed that, one day, men and women would be judged by the content of their character rather than the color of their skin. Dr. King's foundation as a minister was in the Word of God, which establishes worth and dignity for all. But we abandoned that foundation and moved to our own ideas to correct the problem, developing programs like entitlement benefits, diversity training, and affirmative action, along with a myriad of laws. Abandoning Dr. King's focus on character eliminated the very thing that advances any and all people.

Women—in almost all of history, and in some cultures currently—occupy a second-rate status. Efforts to advance their cause is admirable and understandable. I celebrate those accomplishments. I am a practicing dentist in Texas; I'm part of several communities of dentists who are extraordinary people. I am compelled to tell this sad story. Three years ago, a remarkable woman in one of these communities, also a remarkable dentist, took her life. She was struggling to live up to all of the expectations on her life. I find this more often than I would like to. The pressures on a modern-day woman to be a successful professional, a great wife, a great mother, and a whole person is enormous. It got the best of my friend. I know there are many differing views of this, but the pressure remains. The pace of life, demands of life, and complexity of life is a trade-off for the expansion of work life and all the opportunities that come with that life. It is one of the reasons that we see in Generation Y a sincere and heartfelt desire for balance in life and the creation of more time for family and spouses. This shift is encouraging, but as with all things, it can get out of balance as well.

In the most basic sense, for better or worse, in sickness and in health, each individual human being represents the expression of his or her own very unique DNA. To me, an objective look at sexuality begins there. Is there support for the case that sexual identity is determined genetically beyond the obvious male and female characteristics that are expressed in each of us? Examination of literature reveals some work that attempts to establish this. It also reveals the opposite. When you account for the prejudice on both sides of the argument, I believe it is not possible to come to a definitive conclusion. To make a strong case either way, some well-credentialed academic group would need to complete a comprehensive analysis of the peer-reviewed published literature on the subject. Until then, we are stuck with anecdotal statements, stories, and beliefs. To add to all of this is the unprecedented and massive effort by some LGBT leaders to mainstream all forms of sexual identity, lifestyle, and preferences. This effort distorts both the public perception of these issues as well as our general ability to be objective. I will be criticized for simply making that statement, and I risk being labeled a bigot. This is the state of public discourse on the subject of human sexuality today. It is a profound barrier to anyone who genuinely seeks to pursue truth. Changing that would be a great first step. The well-being of millions is at stake. All of this relates to our understanding of human sexuality.

In our postmodern world, one of the basic assumptions is that the chief end of man is the pursuit of *pleasure*. But this ultimately makes life meaningless and requires an individual to construct his or her own life meaning. This conflicts with the classic view that meaning is inherent in each of us as we were created by a God who bestows meaning, purpose, and worth to every individual. Whether intentional or not, the idea of pleasure, comfort, and happiness at almost any cost has been woven into all of life, and especially the sexual revolution of the second turning's effort to create utopia. This idea gave us license and encouragement to experiment with the role of sex in our lives and its importance in our identity. Remember that most if not all the proponents of modernism and postmodernism were motivated, by their own admission, by the freedom they gained in a "God is dead" culture. Without God as a living and breathing part of their life and culture, there was no restraint of their indulgent behavior. Hedonism was not only OK, it was the goal.

As I wrote earlier, Jean-Paul Sartre was one of the most be-

I BELIEVE HE MERELY SOBERED UP FROM A HEDONISTIC LIFE OF INDULGENCE THAT FAILED TO RECONCILE THE OBVIOUS MEANINGLESSNESS OF THAT APPROACH WITH THE ESSENTIAL HUMAN NEED TO UNDERSTAND THE ORIGIN, MEANING, MORALITY, AND DESTINY OF OUR LIVES.

loved writers, philosophers, and thinkers of his day. Sartre, a Frenchman, exhausted himself writing of the nothingness and meaninglessness of life and espousing that pleasure was the only medicine to soothe our souls. He was so wildly successful that, on his death, it was reported that forty thousand young French men and women walked in his funeral procession. But interestingly, on his deathbed, he also recanted his entire worldview and teachings. It was so disturbing to his longtime partner, Simone de Beauvoir, that she thought he had gone mad. I believe he merely sobered up from a hedonistic life of indulgence that failed to reconcile the obvious meaninglessness of that approach with the essential human need to understand the origin, meaning, morality, and destiny of our lives. Although we grow weary of trials, we grow even more disillusioned with a life focused on and filled with pleasure. Pleasure is just too temporary to provide significant satisfaction.

Rarely do we really learn from history well-founded conclusions such as Sartre apparently found—albeit at the end of his life—regarding pleasure. So we turned up the speed of change in the last twenty to thirty years of the sexual revolution. Now we behave, communicate, and legislate as if our sexual identity is the most important aspect of each of our lives. This is so much the case that any different view on sexuality becomes an affront to the very core of a person rather than a conversation about the pros and cons of how we are living and what that means to us individually and collectively. We default to the idea that an extremely active sex life with many different people during the same time period is pleasurable and fun, and we should thus go for it. Or, if we have profound pain from past heterosexual relationships or find love and comfort in homosexual relationships, then that must be where we should turn, that we are gay. Perhaps it does, but shouldn't we take a very long and thorough look at the consequences of that kind of change in our life before we go all in? Our culture would simply answer "go for it" and "if it works for you, then that is how you should live." This is because our culture values pleasure more than nearly anything else. This is the case *even when* we are aware of the intellectual knowledge that pleasure is fleeting and generally leaves us empty afterward. Our essence and our human needs go much deeper than the places pleasure takes us.

Remember, C.S. Lewis said that humans do not have a soul; we *are* a soul. Pleasure is not soulful, at least not soulful enough to satisfy the part of us that feels the deepest and longs for true meaning and hope.

> PLEASURE IS NOT SOULFUL, AT LEAST NOT SOULFUL ENOUGH TO SATISFY THE PART OF US THAT FEELS THE DEEPEST AND LONGS FOR TRUE MEANING AND HOPE.

In recent years we have been asked to believe that homosexuality, bisexuality, and gender identity conflict are genetic developments. Now the same groups are asking us to believe in "sexual fluidity." That means that I can identify as heterosexual today, homosexual next week, or bisexual at a later time. Or that we are simply conflicted about our sexual identity, so we need to surgically and chemically change our state. What will be next? The conflicts in both statements are obvious. And yet, in this postmodern culture that asks us to conform our beliefs, our behaviors, and our relationships to the latest trends, there seems to be no concern about the obvious incoherence. Is that the approach you want your surgeon, bridge engineer, or pilot to take? The only reasons this thinking becomes OK in sexuality is the pure pursuit of pleasure and a relentless desire for self-determinism. We tell ourselves that our experiences, feelings, and desires supersede our actual physical characteristics.

* * * * * * *

How has all of this impacted our view? We have accepted an epidemic of sexually transmitted diseases, many of which are lifelong infections and some of which are lethal. Some prevent future childbirth. Some are precursors to cancer. Since 1973, we have aborted more than 60 million babies in the United States alone. And, as said, in some demographics more than 70 percent of children grow up without a father in single parent households. That is a fast track to poverty, unless the grandparents are there to help.

Sex provides pleasure that is unlike any other human experience. It is intended to do just that. Literally, it is a loving gift from God. That gift is also the mechanism to obey God's command to be fruitful and multiply. The characteristics that come with being male or female help shape our identity, our lives, our behavior, our roles, and the responsibilities that we bear. When those characteristics are conflicted, unclear, or in question, an individual suffers a loss of identity, confusion, and conflict. The pain, it appears, can be debilitating and lead to great despair. Anyone who is in this kind of crisis needs our compassion, understanding, acceptance, and help. But instead of compassionate help, we embrace and celebrate every form of sexual behavior as a fundamental "right" of that conflicted individual to live out, regardless of our factual understanding of what it means for the health and well-being of that individual, their family members, and whoever they would be in a future relationship with! We appear to feel an obligation to not only accept any path that a sexually conflicted person might consider, but that we also must encourage and assist them in their pursuit of sexual goals, up to and including gender change. In addition, some of the LGBT leadership is asking our culture as a whole to reorient employment practices, bathrooms, medical benefits, and many other aspects of day-to-day life for this tiny segment of our population.

Seemingly, we are asked to make such changes without a true understanding of their risks and effects. It is a reflection of how far we have gone in making sexuality the supreme end of a self-determined life. As important as sexuality is, it is *not* the most important aspect of our lives. That error—"total sexual freedom"—introduced in the beginning of the sexual revolution fifty years ago is now magnified beyond all recognition as it has moved, one step at a time, over time, essentially creating new norms. In a postmodern world that essentially rejects standards of all kinds, but especially ethics and morality, how does one begin to consider such "new normals"? It has gone so far that now some parents are unwilling to call a child a boy or girl until they begin to identify that for themselves, regardless of their physical characteristics. That is absolute madness. It is also an open invitation for anxiety, conflict, confusion, and despair in a child.

As with anything that is valuable, our sexuality must be cared for and protected or it will suffer. Protection almost always is accompanied by boundaries, restraint, and a belief that the valuable thing is worth protecting. We have done none of that. Instead of prizing our sexuality, we have bought the Madison Avenue idea that sex sells—and we use sexuality to sell almost everything. We have lived out the sexual revolution, which sought total sexual freedom regardless of the consequences. We are taking the very institutions that a culture is built on and remodeling them to fit our current view of sex and sexuality. But here is yet one more thing to consider: what will we do when we change our minds? Will we remodel our institutions again? In doing so, we have reduced sexuality to the least common denominator of immediate and universal gratification, commercialization, identity creation, and a means to the end of happiness. In this context, happiness is an illusion that is mired in much pain, anxiety, disappointment, and disillusionment. We are designed to give ourselves to one another completely in the context of unconditional love, commitment, protection, and the security that comes from these things. In the absence of those qualities, anxiety, disappointment, disillusionment, and pain appear. And that is a perfect picture of our modern culture.

Here are some summations of what we have discussed in this chapter.

- What we can say about sex and our sexuality is that it is precious and worth protecting. It is a critical part of life, but *not* the most important part. It is intended to play a role in the creation of an abundant life. Today, it is taking us anywhere but in the direction of abundance.

- The fallout from the sexual revolution is tangible, measurable. Sexually transmitted diseases have become increasingly sophisticated, long term, and in some cases deadly. Viruses and bacteria are more intelligent and mutate faster than medicine can adapt. Modern medicine arrogantly and erroneously believed that infectious diseases could be brought under control. They have not.

- The institutions of marriage and family have taken a hit from the sexual revolution in a variety of ways. Divorce became easier; sex outside of marriage expanded. Sex itself has become less tangible and measurable, but it is equally destructive.

- Internet pornography is both an epidemic and a scourge on relationships. It is not abating. Virtual sex is a modern-day illusion. In a postmodern culture where reality is an illusion, Internet sex fits right in. It does not fit relationships and marriages. It destroys them.

- The United States has aborted more than 60 million babies since 1973. One day, I believe, we will look back on our current abortion practices in horror, much like we look back and view the practice of slavery with horror and disgust today.

The expansion and normalization of any and all sexual

practices can't occur without consequences. It is absurd to expect such a result. For every action there is an equal and opposite reaction. The consequences are essentially unlimited in scope and definition.

I wish the fallout of postmodern thought and the utopian-sought sexual revolution had been limited to the tangible and measurable. It has not. In our pursuit of pleasure and happiness we have surrendered joy. Pleasure and happiness became fragile and fleeting. They are dependent upon so many transient and superficial circumstances. True joy lives in our soul. Our soul is a place where we feel the deepest, where we abide in and with our creator. And that place is neither transient, fragile, or fleeting.

Our soul is eternal. It is worth going all in for. Properly developed, your soul can sustain you through your greatest trials and tribulations. In the end, it can take you home. What is more important than that?

ONE TAKEAWAY FROM THIS CHAPTER

What role does sexuality play in your life? Consider these questions.

- Does it define who you are?
- Have you given it more power than it deserves?
- Is your sexuality contributing to abundance or scarcity in your life?

In today's hypersexualized world, our sexual practices often produce moments of pleasure, but moments that are accompanied by equal, or larger, doses of disappointment, emptiness, and anxiety. This is what Jean-Paul Sartre discovered in the end. Do you know those feelings?

NINE

LIGHT

*"This is the message we have heard from
Him and announce to you, that God is light,
and in Him there is no darkness at all."*

—1 JOHN 1:5

I was led to write this book because of the dissonance I observe in the world today. It is as if we have lost the ability to observe the reality that unfolds around us every day, as well as the ability to think logically and productively about those same realities. What gives me the right to claim a more accurate understanding of that reality? To a fault, I am not intuitive. I possess no inherent gifts of insight or vision. However, I do possess the most powerful thing any human can possess. It is available to anyone who is willing. It is a gift from God. That gift is his Spirit, alive in me, that transforms how I experience the world around me and how I understand the message He has declared to each and every one of us. Illumination changes everything.

For the first twenty-five years of my life, my understanding of the world and what was possible for me was determined by myself, my family, and perhaps my community. It all changed when I ran into a problem—actually a very small problem, but one I couldn't fix. I got dumped by a girl. We had been dating for two years. I thought she was going to regret it. She didn't. I did. It was actually the right thing for both of us, but for the first time in my life, I hit the wall. I wasn't sleeping or functioning well. On one of those late nights on a very long run down Memorial Drive in Houston, in an effort to exhaust myself, I finally surrendered.

It went like this. "God, I don't know if you are real or if you are anything like who people say you are. I do know what I am not. I am not strong enough to handle this simple little problem you have given me. I know I can't live this way. If you are real, and you are willing, then I want to trade my life that I am attempting to control for the life that you have for me. I know that I am a mess. I have blown it in a thousand different ways, and I can control very little. So, are you willing?"

I had tried so many times before to bridge that gap, to no avail. The silence was deafening. I had not yet begun to approach the end of myself. This time was different. There was an answer.

There were no fireworks, no astonishing stories, no climactic emotional experiences. There was peace. There was a new beginning. There was a new relationship that layer by layer, day by day, experience by experience would unfold into a life of its own. A new life. There was a promise. It was a one-way eternal covenant from the Creator of the universe. It went like this: "I will put my law within them, and I will write it on their hearts. And I will be their God and they shall be my people" (Jeremiah 31:31, ESV).

In a mysterious, supernatural, and decidedly amazing way, God downloaded the Holy Spirit into my heart, and that light of lights illuminated my journey. It has been messy and often broken, but even in that, it was illuminated by the brightest light of the universe. I see things in a new light. I understand things in a new way. In short, I became a new creature—and none of it was of my ability. I mean none. It was a gift. I put that gift to work by reading, listening, researching, and being influenced by dozens of world-class teachers and thinkers. It has opened up a new world of possibilities. It opened eternity for me.

* * * * * * *

It is late at night. You've just checked into your hotel room. You fumble with, and then get your key card to work, opening the door. You expect an environment you are familiar with, but it is nonetheless entirely new to you. You close the door as you are feeling around the walls for the light switch. It is pitch-black; the blackout drapes are completely closed. Literally, you can see nothing but darkness. Finally, your eyes begin to adjust just a bit to the darkness. Maybe, if it takes long enough to find the light switch, you will begin to pick up very vague images, but essentially you can see nothing. Supposedly, in that room is furniture, carpet, wall coverings, artwork, and all that is typical to a hotel room, but until you can cast light on it, your specific and detailed knowledge is absent or at best speculative and unclear. Then you finally find the light switch, turn it on, and the room is illuminated. Instantly, the reality that is visible before you has changed from pure speculation to a very distinct collection of facts.

Illumination has that effect on us.

Here is the key question: was the reality of that hotel room, its decor and contents, the same regardless of the darkness or the light? Yes, it was. What changed when you turned on the light? What differed was your ability to see what was really present. The ability to see what is really present, not just what we think is present, is life changing. Actually, it is eternity changing.

I believe man's essential problem is that we live in the dark. Mostly, we don't even realize it. We do seem to realize we are missing something. That something drives us to seek answers to overcome the felt separation from the essential reality of our lives and our world. That gap becomes the fuel of worship. It is also what fuels philosophy. Worshipers and philosophers for all of time, knowingly or unknowingly, have been looking for the *quintessence* . . . the fifth essence that unites the four essences of fire, air, water, and earth. As recently as 2014, quantum physicists established the nature of the so-called, long-awaited "God particle," a subatomic particle that is the glue of all matter. Even at the highest level of complexity, in the corridors of science, we still seek unification with the essential reality of our existence.

I BELIEVE MAN'S ESSENTIAL PROBLEM IS THAT WE LIVE IN THE DARK. MOSTLY, WE DON'T EVEN REALIZE IT. WE DO SEEM TO REALIZE WE ARE MISSING SOMETHING.

In this closing chapter, I want to examine how modern and postmodern men and women seek enlightenment. Through what lens do they view the world and ask the most important questions? In essence, how opaque, or transparent, is their lens?[1]

Oliver Sacks, a well-known neurologist, psychologist, and author, described this much better than I ever could. In his book, *Awakenings*, he wrote:

> For all of us have a basic, intuitive feeling that once we were whole and well; at ease, at peace, at home in the world; totally united with the grounds of our being; and then we lost this primal happy innocent state, and fell into our present sickness and suffering. We had something of infinite beauty and preciousness—and we lost

it; we spend our lives searching for what we have lost; and one day, perhaps, we will suddenly find it. And this will be the miracle, the millennium![2]

This is a stunning quote from an agnostic who described nature as his religion. His statement, in different words, is a classic statement of Christian theology and the position of any and every New Testament contributor. Dr. Sacks makes the case that the condition of man is incomplete and separate from this wholeness, peace, and innocence that each of us longs for. Not only that, he claims that each of us intuitively knows we are incomplete in our present state. With these conclusions, I agree.

John, the apostle of Jesus, in the Scripture I began this chapter with, is describing the very nature of God, One that he has seen, heard, and felt. He further claims that he has touched with his own hands the manifestation of God in the flesh in this world—in the form of Jesus. This is an outrageous claim for any human being. John will make even more of them.

The nature of God stands in stark contrast to the nature of man. John, as the ultimate eyewitness, is testifying that the light of God had transformed him and his experience of the world by being the very light that overcomes darkness. The spirit of God in him transformed his ability to see, think, and feel like nothing else. John is categorically stating that this transformation is the way home for each of us.

Many of you will push back hard on John's claim.

So did I.

* * * * * * *

Essential to our quest for completeness and unification is the need to answer four fundamental questions. These questions focus on origin, meaning, morality, and destiny.

Simply stated, these questions ask:

Where did I come from?

What is the purpose of my life?

What are the rules for living with others in this world?

Where am I going after this life?

But the first question, one even before these, is this: from what foundation or reference point will we take our answers? Will they arise from an unchanging point of light that is grounded in eternal truth? Truth that has withstood scrutiny over long periods of time in the marketplace of ideas? Or will it be something we have invented? That "something" is often so attractive to us that we have a hard time not believing it. Mostly, human beings believe in that which is attractive to them. The challenge is navigating through the tension that exists between what is attractive to us and the truth. That is a perilous journey, with more casualties along the way than we can measure.

As we look to reconcile the gap that Sacks described, we seek answers beyond ourselves. This results in worship. Almost every people-group ever studied has found a way to worship something. Mostly, like modern-day Westerners, they had to invent it. Ancient people associated almost every aspect of life with some type of deity who had

THE DARWINIAN EVOLUTIONISTS SAY THAT LIKE ALL SIGNIFICANT TRENDS IN HUMAN EXPERIENCE, WORSHIP SOMEHOW CONTRIBUTES TO THE SURVIVAL OF THE SPECIES. PERHAPS THIS VIEW SEES RELIGIOUS GATHERINGS AND PRACTICES CONTRIBUTING TO A MORE WELL-DEVELOPED SENSE OF COMMUNITY.

domain over some part of their lives. Why? What is it about human beings that drives them to seek the supernatural in worship?

Secularists have several answers. The Darwinian evolutionists say that like all significant trends in human experience, worship somehow contributes to the survival of the species. Perhaps this view sees religious gatherings and practices contributing to a more well-developed sense of community. From that strengthened community comes protection from outside threats of nature and other people-groups. Others, in perhaps a more hostile tone, say that religious belief is for the weak. That believers use it as a crutch. Still others would say established religions become traditions we continue merely out of habit, comfort, or obligation.

In contrast to those ideas, I believe the evidence of human behavior supports the idea that worship is built into our very nature. We all worship something, whether we admit it or not. Atheists and agnostics often worship the intellect of man as the ultimate end. The guys who get painted up on Saturday or Sunday in the colors of their favorite team are worshiping— along with eighty thousand other fans. We worship money, beauty, power, fame, fashion, media celebrities, lying politicians, and sometimes the best things in our world, like our children and grandchildren. By any and every observable measure, we are going to worship. Again, in the words of that great theologian Bob Dylan: "You're gonna serve somebody." Worship does not seem to be optional for human beings.

As we attempt to answer the four questions, we're going to look into the deepest well of life that we are connected to. In an increasingly secular world, those wells can often be dry. The postmodern foundation of meaninglessness does not provide even a basic hope of answers. So, if we are going to go forward with any chance of satisfying our human needs, each of us will need to ask, and seek the answer to, the most important question of our life: ***Does God exist, or did we invent***

Him? Almost every significant belief that we hold will depend on how we answer that question.

How do we find that answer? For many of us, it is automatic. Of course there is a God. How could one think otherwise? Sometimes that is an unexamined assumption that falls apart when life goes south, or when a respected and authoritative person declares differently. Or maybe we just conform to our family's traditions and the expectations of others in continuing that which is comfortable and attractive. But rarely does this provide us answers to the four questions. Rarely does it produce a secure and powerful foundation from which to live.

Secularists have answered the "God question" with a *no*. Secularism views the material world as all that exists. In other words, life is limited to natural events that obey the known scientific laws and principles. In secularism, the supernatural is not possible. Secularism has experienced large growth in the last one hundred years in the West, not so much in the East. It behaves as a religious faith as it attempts to answer the same questions of origin, meaning, morality, and destiny. It just does so in a godless framework. Many secularists would say their religion is nature and the extraordinary beauty and awe they find in the universe. Interestingly, secularists range from the purest Darwinian evolutionists who view the world as survival of the fittest to a secular humanist who lives grounded by and believes in many of the same things a Christian does! Some of the best people I know are secular humanists who are exhausting themselves in their efforts to live the best life possible and become the best people they can. But even those noble efforts do not escape criticism in today's hypercritical world.

European best-selling author John Gray, of The London School of Economics, contrasted these two views of secularism in his book *Straw Dogs*. In it, Gray presents a harsh critique of secular humanists. It is interesting to note that Gray, an outspoken Darwinian evolutionist and passionate atheist, is primarily criticizing fellow secularists as opposed to Christians. As much as I am alarmed by his views, I believe he follows sound logic, taken from his Darwinian basis, in reaching his conclusions. In any case, he writes:

> Darwin showed that humans are like other animals. Humanists claim they are not. Humanists insist that by using our knowledge we can control our environment and flourish as never before. In affirming this, they renew one of Christianity's most dubious promises, that salvation is open to all. The humanist's belief in progress is only a secular version of the Christian faith. In the world shown to us by Darwin, there is nothing that can be called progress. To anyone reared on humanist hopes, this is intolerable. As a result, Darwin's teaching has been stood on its head, and Christianity's cardinal error, that humans are different than all other animals, has been given a new lease on life.[3]

The examples Gray uses in his book are quite difficult to read. The darkness is staggering.

Again, Gray's conclusions and views are alarming and seem like a scary, dehumanizing, futuristic movie. However, if you begin with a Darwinian assumption, as he does, I believe his conclusions are the logical outcome to those assumptions. That is the case regardless of how offensive they are to humanistic people, both secular and God-believing. In my view, Gray strips away what it means to be human in his Darwinian ideology-at-all-costs. He has simply replaced the role of God as Creator, provider, and sustainer of all life with Darwinian theory, his religion.

Within secularism are both atheists and agnostics. Modern-day atheists are a small but vocal group. As such, their voice impacts the culture. They are making enormous efforts to eliminate God from public life and to eliminate each individual's right to publicly express and practice their religious beliefs. Remarkably, those rights include the right of an atheist to publicly express his or her beliefs. Atheism possesses all the characteristics of a religious system.

An atheist is declaring that he has the absolute knowledge that there is no God. The word *atheist* literally means "without God"—*a* means "without," and *theist* is a divine reference. But, logically, for someone to declare absolutely that there is no God, he or she has to possess absolute knowledge of all the universe for all of time. The only being capable of absolute knowledge of all the universe for all known time would be . . . an actual omnipresent, omniscient God. So, being an atheist is actually not logically possible. In essence, the argument falls apart on itself. That does not seem to stop many modern-day atheists from claiming the category. An example of the perspective of a modern-day atheist can be seen in a quote from Dr. Thomas Nagel, a professor at NYU. Nagel wrote:

> LOGICALLY, FOR SOMEONE TO DECLARE ABSOLUTELY THAT THERE IS NO GOD, HE OR SHE HAS TO POSSESS ABSOLUTE KNOWLEDGE OF ALL THE UNIVERSE FOR ALL OF TIME.

> In speaking of the fear of religion I have[,] I don't mean to refer to the entirely reasonable hostility toward certain established religions and religious institutions. That I have in virtue of their objectionable moral doctrines and social policies and political influence. Nor am I referring to the associations of many religious beliefs and superstitions and acceptance of evident empirical falsehoods. I am talking about something much deeper. Namely the fear of religion itself. I speak from experience being strongly subjected to this fear myself[;] I want atheism to be true. I am made uneasy by the fact that some of the most intelligent and well-informed

people that I know are religious believers. It isn't just that I don't believe in God, and naturally hope that I am right in my belief. It is that I hope there is no God. I don't want there to be a God. I don't want the universe to be like that.[4]

That is a powerful and honest admission by Dr. Nagel. I respect his candor.

In contrast, an *agnostic* is making a claim that he or she is without the knowledge of God. The Greek word *gnostos* means "to be known"; again, *a* means "without." An agnostic is saying she has examined the evidence for God and is not convinced of his existence. Although that is not my conclusion, it is a fair conclusion and a growing position as the West becomes more secularized.

The third secular group is perhaps the fastest growing and most telling of our time. I will use the term *functional agnostic* to describe individuals who are essentially apathetic to the concept of a personal God. As baby boomers became more secular, so did their children, those of Generation Y. A secular culture first and foremost is not exposed to the Bible nor educated in its precepts. So all of those ideas become distant and irrelevant. And the even bigger problem is that the individual in this group is making the most important decision of his life, the "God decision," in the dark . . . without being accurately informed of what God has declared in his written Word. This person is informed by the culture around him, the traditions of his family, the opinions of his peers and authority figures, and again, by what looks attractive to him. What that leaves him with is the impact of the wonder and awe of the created universe around him as a general revelation of God to man. Unfortunately, what mostly happens in this case is that people begin to worship the creation rather than finding the Creator.

Another trend adding to this demographic, according to almost all polling and research, is that a large percentage of children who grow up in the church and have been exposed to and educated in basic theology leave the church as adults. They appear to be disillusioned and/or apathetic for a wide variety of reasons. This shift represents one of the most egregious failures of the church. If it is not addressed, this group of functional agnostics will continue to grow and the church will become even more marginalized. The church appears to be positioned at a tipping point—into either renewal and revival or into further marginalization.

> MY QUESTIONS FOR MY AGNOSTIC FRIENDS ARE THESE: HOW THOROUGHLY HAVE YOU LOOKED AT THE EVIDENCE? AND, HOW LONG HAS IT BEEN SINCE YOU LOOKED? ALSO: ARE YOU WILLING TO LOOK AGAIN?

My questions for my agnostic friends are these: how thoroughly have you looked at the evidence? And, how long has it been since you looked? Also: are you willing to look again? Your human needs have not gone away, regardless of how distant they feel.

* * * * * * *

So, how are we to think about the growth of secularism? In other words, looking back at the last one hundred years of history, what fueled the secularization of the West? What historical developments led so many baby boomers into secular lives?

First, the modern and postmodern philosophers **objected to any authority over their lives**. Freedom, especially sexual freedom, was their chief end. Today, our culture essentially demands total freedom.

Second, many people believe **there is a conflict between science and a belief in God**. In reality, science and faith converge on many issues. The issues of the origin of life and the origin of the universe are among the most dramatic that face each of us.

More important than anything else, I believe that many people turn away from a belief in God **because of personal experiences with the church that they find disappointing and painful. There is also all the evil, pain, and suffering we see in the world.**

From that, so many people ask the question: how can there be a loving and all-powerful God when there is so much evil and injustice in this world? That question represents pain that has cut deeply into many of us. It is, clearly, an extremely difficult question to find an adequate answer for. But it does deserves a response.

Of all things, and by all accounts, it appears God has declared love as the most important of all things. That declaration begins with His creation of all things and decision to dwell in His created universe so that we might have the opportunity to have a place in His kingdom and all the eternal blessings that come with it. In addition, the story of man's relationship with God is defined by man's rebellion and God's pursuit of man in spite of his rebellion and rejection. That pursuit continues to this day as God declares His desire for each and every person to know Him and abide in Him. It includes His ultimate provision of Himself as the Messiah to reconcile men and women to Himself. Even if you reject this provision, I believe it is only fair to view it as an unprecedented act of love. It is the most stunning reality that I know.

With love comes choice. To love is to make the choice to love . . . to give of yourself to another. With choice comes the ability to choose good or choose evil. All of us make choices, and many of them, every day. Even when we don't want to, we sometimes make choices that are not in anyone's best interest. Unfortunately, some people seem to totally surrender to evil, and then it is "game on" for the pain, suffering, and injustice that accompanies their choices. Logic tells us that if the only choices available to us were good ones, we would be like robots preprogrammed for specific behaviors and outcomes. That precludes the choice of love. Love requires a great deal of us, including sacrifice.

The foundations of the Judeo-Christian beliefs begin in the book of Genesis. In my view, these accounts provide the best models to explain human behavior. We first read that we are made in God's image according to His likeness. As such, the goodness of God is in each of us and we have something that we call a soul that allows us to supernaturally connect with God. That is one pole. At the other pole, we read the account of the fall of man, in which we turned our backs on God and turned our eyes, hearts, and minds to the world and our own desires. That is the foundation for evil and for our choices to be evil. I propose that each of us lives in the tension between these two poles. Some would refer to that as a dialectic: the conflict of two opposite poles. Living in that tension, each of us will make choices of both types. The apostle Paul, possessing a passionate (even zealot) type of personality, said it best: "For I do not do the good I want to do, but the evil I do not want to do—this I keep on doing" (Romans 7:19, NIV). That describes you and I precisely.

In that tension, the more we surrender to the world and what it has to offer—money, power, fame, sex, drugs, and rock and roll—the more we are choosing evil. Think about sexuality. We start with expanding sexual freedom. Then we expand our sexual choices and partners. Then we focus more of our attention on increasingly erotic experiences, even those that can become criminal. Then we make it an enormous industry; demand is relentless and the consumer motivation immeasurably enormous. That leads to sex trafficking and sexual slavery. It steals the life from young women and young men, literally and figuratively. It kills relationships and creates digital fantasies that are anything but reality. All of this has become the new norm. Any criticism of these new sexual norms is met with ferocious contempt, accusations of bigotry, and overt efforts to restrain speech by law. The words of Sartre have jumped off the pages of his philosophical writings and into real life: "The only thing that is forbidden is to forbid." How much darkness will we endorse?

The amazing thing is that despite man's inhumanity to man throughout history, we don't want to believe it about ourselves. Malcolm Muggeridge, a brilliant British journalist, said this: "The depravity of man is at once the most empirically verifiable reality but at the same time the most intellectually resisted fact."[5]

The evil we object to in the world cannot exist unless it first exists in our hearts. If we are going to push back the darkness that evil is and brings into our world, then we first need to exchange our broken heart for one that is whole.

In this postmodern Western trend, we have created a generic and diluted God who is the compilation of many different pictures. With this kind of framework and mind-set, it is very difficult to discern the character, nature, and very distinct qualities of God. The image of God that we cast with these efforts is very much a blended God who is created from many different human perspectives, rather than His own declaration. Again, we believe in and create a God who is attractive *to us.*

A great example of this came to light in the National Study of Youth and Religion. In 2005, Christian Smith, a highly credentialed and accomplished sociologist at Notre Dame, coauthored a book with Melinda Lundquist Denton that summarized the findings of this study. In their book, they outlined the broad-based religious views of the youth who are now the largest demographic group in the United States: Generation Y. The beliefs they outlined are present both in the established church and outside of it. To summarize the findings, they coined a new term to describe this emerging belief system:

Moralistic Therapeutic Deism.

Smith and Denton described Moralistic Therapeutic Deism as having these five qualities:

1. A god exists who created and ordered the world and watches over human life on earth.

2. God wants people to be good, nice, and fair to each other, as taught in the Bible and by most world religions.

3. The central goal of life is to be happy and to feel good about oneself.

4. God does not need to be particularly involved in one's life except when He is needed to resolve a problem.

5. Good people go to Heaven when they die.[6]

Do these five statements represent the foundational beliefs of any of the world's major religions? The first two, mostly. The last three, not so much. What they really represent is a self-deterministic view of God that is the result of many different cultural trends and behaviors. These views are not built on precepts, evidence, or foundational doctrines.

In asking the "God question," we are really asking the question of what is the ultimate reality. If our answer to the question concerning the reality of God is yes, then that leads to second and third questions: if God exists, has He revealed Himself? And if He has revealed Himself, can we know that revelation? To answer these questions, I believe it would be helpful to compare and contrast some of the major choices that exist in today's world. To be entirely fair to this subject would require an entire book or series of books. I am going to give it a few paragraphs. You can take your personal search as far and as deep as you are willing to go.

* * * * * * *

Historically, Christianity, Islam, Judaism, Hinduism, and Buddhism claimed the most followers. In the West, secularism and New Age belief systems have grown dramatically in the last one hundred years. Although there are many others, we will focus our attention on these seven faiths.

Accompanying growing secularism, New Age, and Eastern beliefs in the Western postmodern world, there is a relentless desire to declare all belief systems equally true, to state that they all say the same things. Perhaps because we have marginalized religious belief in the West, all belief systems are said to be equally irrelevant—or equally quaint—as each of us creates our own reality and our own self-determined truth. So what is true for you is true for you, and what is true for me is true for me. The real sin in this kind of world is declaring that any set of beliefs is superior. You will get worked hard for that today. But doesn't it make sense that it violates the laws of logic to not objectively compare and contrast all of them? Would we leave unexamined any other critical aspect of life? As I have written, would you want your surgeon or bridge engineer to not closely examine their discipline and conform their work to their findings and related standards of truth? Of course not.

WOULD WE LEAVE UNEXAMINED ANY OTHER CRITICAL ASPECT OF LIFE? WOULD YOU WANT YOUR SURGEON OR BRIDGE ENGINEER TO NOT CLOSELY EXAMINE THEIR DISCIPLINE AND CONFORM THEIR WORK TO THEIR FINDINGS AND RELATED STANDARDS OF TRUTH? OF COURSE NOT.

It is possible that all of these belief systems are false, including my own. It is not logically possible that they are all true, as they make exclusive claims that are in conflict with the others. Let's take a look at these claims—and whether, and how, they conflict. We will begin with an easy one before we look at more controversial conflicts as we examine the predominant belief systems.

In **Hinduism** there are many gods, or an impersonal essence. Siddhartha Gautama, the Buddha, grew up in a wealthy, privileged household grounded in Hinduism. At 29 he left his palace and encountered disease, pain, suffering, and injustice for the first time. He saw the caste system of Hinduism as dehumanizing and an essential component of this suffering. To his credit, all of this greatly disturbed him. This led **the Buddha** to reject the teachings of Hinduism, the prominent religion in his nation. He claimed a vision, or visions, in which he concluded that desire was the source of evil in men and women. In this he became an ascetic and taught many concepts designed to help people live noble lives. It is said that his last words were "Never cease striving." He did not directly claim divinity or accept worship. Clearly, with this rejection of the principles of Hinduism by the Buddha in mind, it is not possible to view these two faiths as the same. Although both are Eastern belief systems, they differ in their essential messages about man, the divine, and the nature of reincarnation.

In **Islam**, the most monotheistic of all faiths, there is a creator who is elevated to such a lofty status that he is personally unknowable. He spoke through his singular messenger, Mohammed, to whom he gave his revelation. Islam states that there is one God, Allah, and that his messenger is Mohammed. Foundational in Islam is the view of Mohammed that the Scriptures of Christianity and Judaism had been corrupted from their early, accurate state. Mohammed claimed these Scriptures were in error. However, neither Mohammed, nor subsequent leaders and scholars, presented any earlier manuscripts we can use to compare and contrast the Old Testament or New Testament manuscripts. Without earlier documents to establish their error claim, it remains unsubstantiated. In addition, both Judaism and Christianity view their Scriptures as God-inspired, accurate, essential, complete, and the foundation of each faith. Further, the Quran and the Bible describe the character and nature of God in two completely different ways.

Finally, Islam is an Eastern belief system. It is not limited to a religious faith but rather is a construct of religious belief, government, culture, and law. It is in this construct that we find enormous difficulty in integrating Islamic people into Western democracies. Western nations are not theocracies. For a Muslim to live out all of the construct of Islam requires that Islamic religious belief, culture, government, and law merge into one whole. That defines a theocracy. For a Muslim to integrate into Western cultures, he or she has to leave behind at least part of the Islamic construct. That is extremely difficult to do when that system has represented all of life to them for all of their lives.

Jewish law is interested in ruling the lives of Jews. Christianity freed its followers of the law and is interested in the condition of each individual's soul, regardless of the culture, government, or law. Neither Judaism nor Christianity speaks to ruling a nation or its culture. They cannot be the same as Islam.

The ultimate reality of **Christianity** and **Judaism** is a Creator who is personal, available to all men and women, and has made Himself known. The Creator has provided for, pursued, and had direct contact with men and women since their creation.

Jews and Christians differ over the central issue

THE DIFFERENCE BETWEEN THE TWO BELIEFS IS IRRECONCILABLE. THEY CANNOT BE THE SAME. OF COURSE, THE IRONY IN ALL OF THIS IS THAT JESUS IS A JEW.

of Jesus as the long-expected Jewish Messiah. If he is not the Messiah, then Christians are committing heresy by worshipping a false god and violating God's commandment that "you shall have no other gods but me." If He is the Messiah, then Jews have rejected God himself. The difference between the two beliefs is irreconcilable. They cannot be the same. Of course, the irony in all of this is that Jesus is a Jew. In addition, sixty-four of the sixty-six books in the Christian Bible were written by Jews. (Luke and Acts, both written by Luke, a Gentile doctor, are the exceptions.) So Christians and Jews are irreconcilably different but, at the same time, eternally connected and interdependent. Christians are called to support Israel and pursue whatever unity is possible with the Jewish people. In God's covenant with Abraham, God declared this clearly and powerfully.

> *"And I will bless those who bless you,*
> *And the one who curses you, I will curse. And in you*
> *all the families of the earth will be blessed."*
> —Genesis 12:3 (NASB)

Finally, we find the newest construct of religious belief in a modern-day version of pantheism, which means god in all things, and monism, meaning god is one, in the development of **New Age** teachings. The believers in this system mostly describe their views as "spirituality" rather than actually calling it New Age. It takes its name from a belief in a coming utopian age. Its central truth is of a divine oneness, or God, in all things. The basic beliefs of the New Age movement come from Hinduism and Buddhism. Those Eastern ideas came to life in the United States in the early 1900s through the voices of Swami Vivekenanda, Paramahansa Yogananda, Maharishi Mahesh Yogi, and others.

Frederick Nietzsche led the "God is dead" movement in the late 1800s in Europe, beginning the intellectual elimination of God from our culture. So the New Age movement was the perfect storm to follow the "death of God" in the West. It brought an impersonal spirituality to replace the concept of a personal God with authority to whom we are accountable. The "divine oneness," or God-in-all-things belief, meant that we were unconditionally connected to, and emanated from, God, in all ways and for all of time. Essentially, there is no separation from oneness in God if we just accept that "truth." Human pursuit of contact with the supernatural through "channeling" is often a component of this religious system. To my knowledge, there are no foundational scriptures for New Age beyond the Vedas of Hinduism written in ancient India and the writings of the Buddha. The remaining writings are current commentary from a variety of individuals and influences. Deepak Chopra is a very well-known voice of New Age spirituality. There are a wide variety of practices and priorities in this belief system.

As you have heard and read many times, nature abhors a vacuum. The death of God in Western culture left a void. Some of that void was filled with the secular beliefs of modernism and postmodernism. Some of it was filled with the eastern beliefs of New Age spirituality. Islam is attempting to fill a very stark vacuum of faith in Europe. Many Muslims hope for *sharia*, the complete rule of Islamic law in the world. To this end, Muslims are seeking more converts, attacking other religious systems both by the sword and by word, moving into every nation, and seeking political power wherever they can achieve it. Islam is a growing and aggressive religion that seeks to submit everyone on the planet to its rule.

If religious systems and efforts are intended to bring illumination, understanding, and hope to human beings . . . to fill the voids in our hearts . . . to shine light on the darkness . . . to bring real hope . . . we must ask the question: are they doing that? The state of the world says no. The behavior of many of the followers say no. So how are we to think about all of this?

What are we to do to combat the darkness of the world and these belief systems?

* * * * * * *

Some of the darkest places in the world are, at the same time, in the midst of revolution. People in places that you would never dream of seeking and finding the God of all creation are doing just that. Or, perhaps, *He* is finding *them*. This is a revolution in search of light. It is a revolution that has met and is meeting unprecedented resistance. The resistance is losing.

Mao Zedong, Chaiman Mao, began revolutionary activities in China around 1917; his movement culminated in the founding of the Peoples Republic of China in 1949. In taking total control of China, Mao was responsible for an estimated 40 million to 70 million deaths through starvation, forced labor, and executions, ranking his tenure as the top incidence of democide (defined, quite simply, as murder by government) in human history. He also took control of the Christian church in China. Mao said that he was going to kill it. He tried. He closed the churches, seminaries, schools, and orphanages. He burned the Bibles and all of Christian literature that he could. He deported all the missionaries. Mao arrested, tortured, and executed countless numbers of Chinese Christians who refused to renounce their faith. Since then, in essence, the Christian church has been outlawed. All of that history would make you think the Christian church is dead in China. It is anything but. It is estimated that by 2050 there will be more followers of Jesus Christ in China than any nation on earth.

Africa has seen an explosion of Christian belief. According to the Pew Research Center's report on global Christianity, 23.6 percent of the world's 2 billion Christians live in Sub-Saharan Africa. That is stunning. Asia has 13.1 percent, the Americas 36.8 percent, Europe 25.9 percent, and the Middle

East/North Africa .6 percent. The world has changed in the last one hundred years. In the West, we think that Christianity is dying. It isn't. It's just moving.

Mao, Voltaire, Nietzsche, Lenin, Stalin, and so many others made the same mistake. They believed that human efforts, human thought, and human belief could kill God. Laws may limit human behavior.

THE WORLD HAS CHANGED IN THE LAST ONE HUNDRED YEARS. IN THE WEST, WE THINK THAT CHRISTIANITY IS DYING. IT ISN'T. IT'S JUST MOVING.

But those laws and human efforts are irrelevant to a God who created the universe. If God is truly who the Bible and 2 billion people claim Him to be, who is going to derail His plan for mankind, individually and collectively? The answer is, of course, nobody.

In considering the many and varied belief systems available to each of us, a number of important things stand out.

First, in the West we have the freedom to pursue any and all beliefs. We are free to worship or not worship as we see fit as long as we are not blatantly harming another person. Disagreement is not harm, it is just disagreement. I have been in nations where the people are not free to know anything other than the dominant belief held in that nation. That makes me extremely sad.

Second, the contrast between the world's religions is stunning. Islam presents a monotheistic view in which God is supremely elevated and authoritative. A place in Allah's kingdom depends on an individual surrendering to that idea and their good deeds outweighing their bad ones. In a completely opposite framework, Hinduism has millions of gods. It embraces a wide variety of viewpoints. Buddhism does not teach a personal God, and the Buddha did not accept worship as a God would. He taught many wise things for living in this world. Both Hinduism and Buddhism teach reincarnation, in different forms, as the path of reward or punishment depending on the life you have lived. New Age beliefs that arose from both of these Eastern religions does not teach a personal God, but paints with a broad brush a God-in-all-things so that the only separation between man and God is the errant perception by man that the separation existed in the first place. Reconciliation requires understanding this and accepting your rightful connection to God.

Secularism coming of age in modern and postmodern thought rejects the idea of God altogether. By the admission of virtually every major philosopher proposing completely secular ideas, the logical conclusion to a godless world is . . . that all things are essentially meaninglessness. Eliminating God eliminates the source of truth, meaning, and morality. Each person decides for himself or herself what is right and wrong. That is the very definition of darkness.

In contrast to all of these religions stands one figure who brings a completely different message, Jesus of Nazareth. This man made the most outrageous statements of all time.

In John 8:58 Jesus claimed to be God: "Jesus said to them, 'Truly, truly, I say to you, before Abraham was born, I Am.'" The "I Am" reference comes from Exodus 3:14 in the Old Testament Scriptures, where God said to Moses, "I AM WHO I AM. Thus you shall say to the sons of Israel: I AM has sent me to you." Jesus will make this same claim many times and in many different ways.

In John 11:25 Jesus claimed to be the provider of eternal life. He said to a woman named Martha: "I am the resurrection and the life; he who believes in me will live even if he dies." He would go on to say, in many different ways, that He did not come to make bad people good but to make dead people alive. He did this by offering them a way to God.

Perhaps the most offensive statement to a self-deterministic world comes in Jesus' words in John 14:6. This conversation came less than twenty-four hours before Jesus' death. He was doing what all great leaders do, preparing His followers for what was to come. They were scared and confused. He said to them: "Do not let your hearts be troubled." He was telling them that He was going to prepare a place for them where they would be reunited. You can imagine that His words did not sound nearly concrete enough to help them in their fear. His disciples had given up their lives, families, and careers to follow Him. And after three years of controversy, miracles, teaching, and transformation they knew it was all about to change. They had one central question: After all we have been through, can you still get us home? Can we count on you? When he said to them, "And you know the way where I am going," it was just too much for Thomas! This was the same doubting Thomas who readers of Scripture know is always looking for clarity, confirmation, and security. He said, "We do not know where you are going, so how do we know the way?" It was then, in the midst of chaos, confusion, and fear that Jesus spoke the ultimate reality of His being. To Thomas, and all disciples, he said, "I am the way and the truth and the life; no one comes to the Father but through me" (14:6). He did not say that He would show them the way. He did not say that God had revealed to Him the way. He did not say that He had discovered the way. He said, "I *am* the way." It's all on me, He seemed to be saying. I will get you home, period. No one before or since has *ever* made that promise and kept it—except Jesus, who claims to be the Savior of the world.

* * * * * * *

We don't want the world to be a place that is defined by injustice, suffering, and pain, but all too often it is. We don't want the human heart to be a place that is corrupt, but if you could read my mind and view every thought I have, you would realize that all too often it is filled with unwanted corruption, disappointment, and despair. It is also filled with great things at times, but the tension between the two poles can be overwhelming. And, I imagine, if I could view your thoughts, I would see much the same.

The cure for the disease of darkness is obviously *light*. When you open your front door at night, the darkness does not rush in, the light rushes out—to illuminate. Light always pushes back the darkness. That is exactly what Jesus does in my heart, and what He can do in yours.

Once again, the apostle John, in 8:4-11 of his book, records one of the greatest testimonies to the light of the world. The Pharisees were trying to trap Jesus into violating the law with His statements. Did they really think they could outsmart God? Apparently, they did. They dragged a woman before Jesus and then flung her to the ground before Him. Here is what transpired.

> "Teacher, this woman has been caught in adultery, in the very act. Now in the Law Moses commanded us to stone such women; what then do you say?" They were saying this, testing Him, so that they might have grounds for accusing Him. But Jesus stooped down and with His finger wrote on the ground. But when they persisted in asking Him, He straightened up, and said to them, "He who is without sin among you, let him be the first to throw a stone at her." Again He stooped down and wrote on the ground. When they heard it, they began to go out one by one, beginning with the older ones, and He was left alone, and the woman, where she was, in the center of the court. Straightening up, Jesus said to her, "Woman, where are they? Did no one condemn you?" She said, "No one, Lord." And Jesus said, "I do not condemn you, either. Go. From now on sin no more."

I often wonder how the religious leaders knew exactly where to find her. Perhaps they had visited her place before. Perhaps not. In any case, they were clearly showing their hand

as they used their position, power, authority, and the law itself to condemn a woman just to combat the threat that Jesus
brought them. But when confronted with the reality of their
own lives, one by one they dropped each stone and walked
away, convicted of their own sin and no longer the woman's.
It is exactly what happens when the mind of man does battle
with the mind of God.

In what was a stunning act of grace and kindness, the only
person with the authority to judge this woman . . . did not.
Instead, Jesus offered her forgiveness, not condemnation, and
He gave her life instead of death. He offers the same to you
and me: unconditional forgiveness, unconditional acceptance,
unconditional love, and life instead of death.

In this remarkable story and in every moment of every day
in every part of the world, Jesus pushes back the darkness and
calls you and I into His fellowship. He is the light of the world.

ONE TAKEAWAY FROM THIS CHAPTER

What is your call to be light in this world? What are
your gifts that God has given you? Begin with these simple questions. Journal. Talk to trusted friends. Pray. Then
begin to use your gifts. God has given you His light for
His purposes.

EPILOGUE

Entropy is a scientific term that represents a principle of statistical thermodynamics. Simply put, it says that matter moves from higher order to lower order. In real-life terms: iron rusts. Entropy is a description of, or measure of, disorder. Any idea or scientific theory that challenges the relentless power of entropy, to establish itself, is destined to fail.

Life systems possess their own unique version of entropy. DNA, RNA, and related systems serve as exquisitely precise instruction sets for building proteins for all biochemical systems required by a cell for life. Living beings are constantly exposed to ultraviolet radiation from the sun and other environmental factors and, by necessity, burn fuel to live. Therefore, their DNA is subject to damage from oxidative stress. In that damage, the instruction sets in the DNA begin to slowly break down and become more disordered. We build better and more highly ordered cells earlier in life and less robust and more disordered cells as we age. You already know this unless you are very young. The biology of life is subject to entropy. It is relentless.

Why the short discussion on entropy? *Unchanging Points of Light* is a collection of ideas about social entropy. Social entropy is a measure of the natural decay within a social system. It implies the tendency of social networks and society in general to break down over time, moving from cooperation and advancement toward conflict and chaos. The concepts of truth, life, love, identity, race, money, power, sexuality, and the power of illumination are the building blocks and fuel of the social systems of our culture. Initially, the disorder introduced into the system is barely noticeable. But as the disorder progresses toward the limits of the system, it overtakes and overwhelms the social systems and structures that are so critical to an abundant, stable, and prosperous society. At their limits, they break down.

In describing this, I attempted to create contrast and specificity around the meaning associated with each idea. This came with the hope that these ideas would shine so brightly and with such clarity that you could grasp them well enough to act on them. But how can one possibly defy the relentless nature of entropy, especially when this world tends to take all that we are and all that we have just to survive?

The power you need, however, doesn't come from this world. It comes from another world. It came in the form of a man who lived two thousand years ago. He defines order. He created the universe and every detail of every cell that is every living thing to an ordered complexity beyond human comprehension. There is nothing that is beyond His power.

He said this to His disciples in a moment when they couldn't find the power they needed:

"If you can? Everything is possible to him that believes"

(MARK 9:23, NIV).

He created the universe. He chose to dwell in that universe. He chose to come to this earth and become human. In His human form, He gave everything He had to give for you and me because He loves us more than we have the capacity to comprehend.

There is nothing impossible to Him—nothing. With Him, you can take on the most powerful forces in the universe—even the entropy of social forces—and win.

ENDNOTES

TRUTH

1. Alexis G. Burgess and John P. Burgess, *Truth* (Princeton University Press, 2011).

2. occupywallst.org (accessed: October 1, 2016).

3. Isaiah 1:5-7, New American Standard Bible.

LIFE

1. ted.com, Alexander Tsiaras, "Conception to Birth Visualized," December 2010, http://www.ted.com/talks/alexander_tsiaras_conception_to_birth_visualized (accessed November 23, 2016).

2. genome.gov. A comprehensive overview of the Human Genome Project can be read here. Clinton remarks: https://www.genome.gov/10001356/june-2000-white-house-event/june-2000-white-house-event/ (accessed November 25, 2016).

3. Paul Davies, *The Fifth Miracle: The Search for the Origin and Meaning of Life* (Simon & Shuster, 1999).

4. The Miller-Urey Experiment: Amino Acids and The Origins of Life on Earth, juliantrubin.com (accessed October 1, 2016).

5. McLean v. Arkansas Board of Education. U.S. District Court Judge William R. Overton handed down the decision in favor of the plaintiff, January 5, 1982. Published in *Science*, February 19, 1982. http://www.panspermia.org/chandra.htm (accessed December 8, 2016).

6. Atul Gawande, *The Checklist Manifesto* (Metropolitan Books, 2009).

7. petersinger.info (accessed: October 1, 2016).

LOVE

1. Frank Dobbin and Alexandra Kalev, "Why Diversity Programs Fail," *Harvard Business Review,* July-August 2016.

2. Ibid.

3. Ibid.

4. Gardiner Morse, "Designing a Bias-Free Organization," *Harvard Business Review*, July-August 2016, 63-67.

5. Dobbin and Kalev.

IDENTITY

1. Bob Dylan, "Gotta Serve Somebody," © Special Rider Music, Bob Dylan, from: *Slow Train Coming* (1979); http://bobdylan.com/songs/gotta-serve-somebody/ (accessed December 7, 2016).

2. Materials for this chapter also came from the Institute for American Values, "Hardwired to Connect: The New Scientific Case for Authoritative Communities" (2003).

MONEY

1. Board of Governors of the Federal Reserve System, "Report on the Economic Well-Being of U.S. Households in 2015," May 2016.

2. William Strauss and Neil Howe, *The Fourth Turning* (Penguin Random House, 1996).

POWER

1. Victor Frankl, *Man's Search For Meaning* (Simon & Shuster, 1984).

2. Valuable material regarding Bonhoeffer's life can be found in: Eric Metaxas, *7 Men: And the Secret of their Greatness* (Thomas Nelson, 2013).

3. The Center for Security Policy Press, "Catastrophic Failure: Blindfolding America in the Face of Jihad," 2015.

4. William J. Federer, *What Every American Needs to Know About the Qur'an: A History of Islam and the United States* (Amerisearch, 2007).

5. Nabeel Qureshi, *Answering Jihad: A Better Way Forward* (Zondervan, 2016).

6. Isaiah 42:1-4, New International Version.

7. Joe D. Batten, *Tough-Minded Leadership* (Amacom Books, 1989).

SEXUALITY

1. C.S. Lewis, *Surprised by Joy: The Shape of My Early Life* (Harcourt, Brace, Jovanovich, 1966).

2. Sir Thomas More, *Utopia* (Penguin Classics, 2003).

3. http://www.merriam-webster.com/dictionary/utopia (accessed November 16, 2016).

4. Ibid.

LIGHT

1. Valuable material in this chapter is owed to: Dean C. Halverson, *The Compact Guide to World Religions* (Bethany House, 1996).

2. Oliver Sacks, *Awakenings* (Random House, 1973), 28.

3. John Gray, *Straw Dogs: Thoughts on Humans and Other Animals* (Granta Books, 2004).

4. Thomas Nagel, *The Last Word* (Oxford University Press, 1997).

5. Malcom Muggeridge, edited by Ian A. Hunter, *The Very Best of Malcom Muggeridge* (Regent College Publishing, 2003).

6. Christian Smith with Melinda Denton, *Soul Searching: The Religious and Spiritual Lives of American Teenagers* (Oxford University Press, 2009).

ABOUT THE AUTHOR

Edwin A. McDonald III is more than fine when his patients call him Dr. Mac or even just "Mac." He is a general dentist whose practice is grounded in developing trusting relationships—which he thinks of as partnerships—with his patients and the talented team of professionals he collaborates with. The focus of his practice is managing complex dental problems that require esthetic and functional correction. "I love what I do and how I get to do it," he says.

Dr. Mac is a graduate of Midwestern State University (BS, chemistry) and has a DDS from the University of Texas (Houston Dental Branch). He has completed extensive postgraduate training in esthetic, restorative, and implant dentistry. He is a visiting faculty member at the Pankey Institute in Key Biscayne, Florida and at Spear Education in Scottsdale, Arizona. He was chairman of the Southwest Dental Conference in Dallas in 2015 and will serve as chairman of the annual session of the Texas Dental Association in 2019.

Dr. Mac is a lifelong learner and now a teacher, mentor, and frequent lecturer at major professional meetings across the United States. He lectures on clinical subjects as well as team building, leadership, and management. He is a student in the Naveen Jindal School of Management of the University of Texas at Dallas pursuing a certificate in executive and professional coaching. His plan is to begin coaching professionals toward more abundant and rewarding careers.

A long run in the middle of a sleepless night as a senior in dental school is when Mac began his journey as a follower of Christ. That journey quickly included pursuit of Christian apologetics. Much of this book comes from thirty years of reading and listening to the best of the best in apologetics, philosophy, culture, and science. Dr. Mac believes there is no better time in all of history to ask the most difficult and important questions about our lives and our world. Of course there is and always will be great mystery fueling our imagination, speculation, and conversations. However, at the same time, more empirical data describing the world's cultures exists than ever before.

He believes there is no reason to live in the dark concerning these subjects. Shining a bright light on them is the reason for this book, and the reason for much of his future work.